Cupcakes & Muffins

This edition published in 2013
LOVE FOOD is an imprint of Parragon Books Ltd

Parragon
Chartist House
15–17 Trim Street
Bath, BA1 1HA, UK

ISBN: 978-1-4454-7319-2

Printed in China

Created and produced by Ivy Contract
Photography by Sian Irvine
Food styling by Jack Sargeson, Anna Irvine and Maud Eden
New recipes by Susanna Tee with Sarah Banberry and Jacqueline Bellefontaine

Notes for the Reader
This book uses both metric and imperial measurements. Follow the same
units of measurement throughout; do not mix metric and imperial. All spoon
measurements are level: teaspoons are assumed to be 5 ml, and tablespoons are
assumed to be 15 ml. Unless otherwise stated, milk is assumed to be full fat, eggs
and individual vegetables are medium, and pepper is freshly ground black pepper.

Garnishes, decorations and serving suggestions are all optional and not necessarily
included in the recipe ingredients or method.

The times given are an approximate guide only. Preparation times differ according
to the techniques used by different people and the cooking times may also vary
from those given. Optional ingredients, variations or serving suggestions have not
been included in the time calculations.

Recipes using raw or very lightly cooked eggs should be avoided by infants, the
elderly, pregnant women, convalescents and anyone suffering from an illness.
Pregnant and breastfeeding women are advised to avoid eating peanuts and peanut
products. Sufferers from nut allergies should be aware that some of the ready-
made ingredients used in the recipes in this book may contain nuts. Always check
the packaging before use.

Cupcakes
& Muffins

A collection of 200 delicious recipes

Contents

Introduction

The cupcakes and muffins included in this book are easy and enjoyable to make, fun to eat and great to share whatever the time of day. They are the perfect choice for a midmorning coffee or afternoon tea, at a children's party or on a festive occasion. Whatever the reason, you are sure to find what you are looking for among the delicious goodies that have been gathered together in this collection.

The star ingredients

Sugar, fat, eggs, flour and a liquid are the basic ingredients that the majority of the recipes share.

Sugar

Caster sugar is usually recommended because it dissolves more easily than granulated sugar. Nevertheless, granulated sugar can be used if necessary.

Fat

Butter is the fat that is suggested in most of the recipes, as this adds richness and gives the best flavour. However, margarine can be used as an alternative, and is less expensive. It is

important, though, to use a margarine containing not less than 60 per cent fat; choose a hard margarine that is described on the packet as suitable for baking. The exception is when a recipe calls for a soft margarine. In this instance all the ingredients are beaten together with an electric mixer until mixed.

Eggs

The size of eggs used in the recipes is medium unless otherwise stated. If possible, use eggs that are at room temperature because cold eggs can cause the mixture to curdle and will result in a less soft mixture.

Flour

The flour used in the recipes may be plain or self-raising. Should you need self-raising flour but only have plain, sift 2½ teaspoons of baking powder into every 225 g/8 oz plain flour.

Liquid

The liquid in the recipes is used to bind the ingredients together and is usually milk, eggs, butter, oil, water or fruit juice.

Assuring success

Almost all the recipes in the book are easy to make. Follow these useful suggestions and you will be guaranteed success every time you bake:

● Preheat the oven for 10–15 minutes before baking, even if the oven manufacturer's instructions suggest that this is not necessary. If you have a fan-assisted oven, reduce the temperature according to their instructions.

● It is important that ingredients are measured accurately, so it is worth investing in good-quality scales and standard measuring spoons.

● Get into the habit of preparing paper cases and tins before commencing preparation, as mixtures that contain self-raising flour start to activate once the liquid has been added to them and should therefore be baked as soon as possible after they have been prepared.

● It is not necessary to sift flour unless you are combining several dry ingredients to facilitate even mixing.

● When butter or hard margarine needs to be softened before blending with another ingredient, either remove it from the refrigerator and leave at room temperature for about 1 hour, or cut into cubes, place in a bowl and microwave on High for 10 seconds, until softened slightly. Be careful not to allow it to melt.

● After adding the flour to a mixture, do not overbeat it as this will make the mixture tough.

● Position baking trays on the middle rack of the oven for even browning.

● Unless otherwise stated, transfer cupcakes and muffins to a wire rack directly after they are removed from the oven, and leave to cool. This will allow the steam to evaporate and prevent them from becoming soggy.

● When baking, try to resist the temptation to open the oven door during the first half of the cooking time as cold air can cause the mixture to sink in the middle.

Equipment & helpful techniques

Making any of the recipes in this book requires very little special equipment and, in many cases, improvisation can be helpful! Nevertheless, here are some suggestions that you may find useful:

● If a recipe asks for toasted nuts and you do not have any, you can toast them yourself. Preheat the oven to 180°C/350°F/ Gas Mark 4. Spread the nuts in a single layer on a baking sheet and cook in the preheated oven for 5–10 minutes, turning and watching them carefully until golden brown.

● Many of the recipes require you to melt chocolate in a heatproof bowl set over a saucepan of simmering water. This is the safest way to melt it because it will not overheat and become dry. Make sure the bowl does not touch the water. You can also melt chocolate in a microwave. To do this, break the chocolate into a heatproof bowl and cook on Low until the chocolate is soft on top. As a guide, 100 g/3½ oz will take about 4 minutes. Check and stir every minute.

● With a few exceptions, most of the recipes in this book will keep well in a tin or airtight container.

● Ideally, store baked cupcakes and muffins undecorated. Any item that is decorated with cream, cream cheese or yogurt should be stored in the refrigerator.

● Most cupcakes and muffins can be frozen and thawed at short notice, but most are best when just baked.

The finishing touches

Glacé icing

115 g/4 oz icing sugar
1 tbsp cold water

Sift the sugar into a bowl and gradually add the water, then beat together until the icing coats the back of a spoon.

American frosting

225 g/8 oz caster sugar
4 tbsp water
¼ tsp cream of tartar
½ tsp vanilla extract
1 egg white

Place the sugar, water and cream of tartar into a saucepan and heat gently until the sugar has dissolved. Add the vanilla and heat (without boiling), stirring until the temperature reads 120°C/250°F on a sugar thermometer. Cool slightly. Whisk the egg white in a large bowl until stiff, then continue whisking as you add the syrup in a thin stream and until it is smooth and thick.

Chocolate frosting

100 g/3½ oz plain chocolate, chopped
140 g/5 oz butter, softened
140 g/5 oz icing sugar
½ tsp chocolate extract

Place the chocolate in a heatproof bowl, set the bowl over a saucepan of gently simmering water until melted. Cool. Beat the butter in a bowl until fluffy, then sift in the sugar and beat until smooth. Add the cooled chocolate and chocolate extract and beat until combined.

Buttercream

225 g/8 oz butter, softened
1 tbsp cream or milk
350 g/12 oz icing sugar
Note To make chocolate buttercream,
*   substitute 50 g/1¾ oz cocoa for sugar*

Place the butter and cream in a bowl and beat together. Gradually sift in the icing sugar and beat until smooth.

Fondant icing

500 g/1 lb 2 oz icing sugar
1 egg white
2 tbsp liquid glycerin
1 tsp vanilla extract or almond extract

Sift the icing sugar into a large bowl and gradually beat in the egg white until the mixture is thick and smooth. Beat in the glycerin and vanilla extract.

Cream cheese icing

125 g/4½ oz butter, softened
225 g/8 oz cream cheese
450 g/1 lb icing sugar
1 tsp vanilla extract

Place the butter and cheese in a bowl and beat until light and fluffy. Gradually sift in the sugar, add the vanilla and beat until smooth.

Iced cupcakes

> 115 g/4 oz butter, softened
> 115 g/4 oz caster sugar
> 2 eggs, lightly beaten
> 115 g/4 oz self-raising flour
>
> TOPPING
> 200 g/7 oz icing sugar
> about 2 tbsp warm water
> a few drops of food colouring (optional)
> sugar flowers, hundreds and thousands,
>   glacé cherries and/or chocolate
>   strands, to decorate

Preheat the oven to 190°C/375°F/Gas Mark 5. Line two 12-hole bun tins with 16 paper cases. Place the butter and sugar in a large bowl and beat together until light and fluffy, then gradually beat in the eggs. Sift in the flour and fold into the mixture. Spoon the mixture into the paper cases.

Bake in the preheated oven for 15–20 minutes. Transfer to a wire rack to cool completely.

To make the icing, sift the icing sugar into a bowl and stir in just enough warm water to mix to a smooth paste that is thick enough to coat the back of a wooden spoon. Stir in a few drops of food colouring, if using, then spread the icing over the cupcakes and decorate, as liked.

02 Orange cupcakes

Add the grated rind of ½ orange to the cake mixture after beating in the eggs. Use orange juice instead of water when making the icing.

03 Lemon cupcakes

Add the grated rind of ½ lemon to the cake mixture after beating in the eggs. Use lemon juice instead of water when making the icing.

04 Chocolate cupcakes

Replace 2 tablespoons of the flour with 2 tablespoons of cocoa and add 2 teaspoons of cocoa to the icing sugar when making the icing.

05 Coffee cupcakes

Dissolve 2 tablespoons of instant coffee in 3 tablespoons of boiling water. Add about two thirds to the cake mixture after beating the eggs. Add the remainder to the icing sugar when making the icing.

06 Mocha cupcakes

Dissolve 1 tablespoon of instant coffee in 2 tablespoons of boiling water and beat in after adding the eggs. Add 1 tablespoon of cocoa to the flour and fold in. For a mocha icing, add 1 teaspoon of cocoa to the icing sugar. Dissolve 1 teaspoon of instant coffee in 1 tablespoon of boiling water and stir into the icing sugar mixture with enough water until smooth.

07 Almond cupcakes

Add 1 teaspoon of almond extract after beating in the eggs. Replace 2 tablespoons of the flour with ground almonds.

08 Nutty cupcakes

Add 40 g/1½ oz finely chopped walnuts, pecan nuts or toasted hazelnuts before folding in the flour.

140 g/5 oz butter, softened,
    or soft margarine
140 g/5 oz caster sugar
1½ tsp vanilla extract
2 eggs, lightly beaten
200 g/7 oz self-raising flour

TOPPING
1 quantity buttercream (page 8)
a selection of classic small sweets, such
    as jelly beans, to decorate

Preheat the oven to 190°C/375°/Gas Mark 5. Line two 12-hole bun tins with 18 paper cases. Place the butter and sugar in a large bowl and beat together until light and fluffy, then beat in the vanilla extract. Gradually beat in the eggs, then sift in the flour and fold into the mixture. Spoon the mixture into the paper cases.

Bake in the preheated oven for 12–15 minutes, or until golden and springy to the touch. Transfer to a wire rack to cool completely.

Place the buttercream in a piping bag fitted with a small star nozzle and pipe the buttercream on top of each cake. Arrange the sweets on top to decorate.

10 *Sweet-topped chocolate cupcakes*

Reduce the vanilla extract to ½ teaspoon. Melt 70 g/2½ oz plain chocolate, broken into pieces, and stir into the cake mixture after beating in the eggs. Decorate with chocolate buttercream (page 8) and small chocolate sweets.

11 *Birthday party cakes*   MAKES 24

225 g/8 oz butter, softened, or soft
    margarine
225 g/8 oz caster sugar
4 eggs
225 g/8 oz self-rising flour

TOPPING
175 g/6 oz butter, softened
350 g/12 oz icing sugar

a variety of sweets and chocolates, sugar-
    coated chocolates, dried fruits, edible
    sugar flower shapes, cake decorating
    sprinkles, sugar strands, silver or gold
    dragées, hundreds and thousands,
    various tubes of coloured writing icing
    and candles and candleholders
    (optional), to decorate

Preheat the oven to 180°C/350°F/Gas Mark 4. Line two 12-hole bun tins with 24 paper cases. Place the butter, sugar, eggs and flour in a large bowl and beat together until just smooth. Spoon the mixture into the paper cases.

Bake in the preheated oven for 15–20 minutes, or until well risen, golden brown and firm to the touch. Transfer to a wire rack to cool.

To make the icing, place the butter in a bowl and beat until fluffy. Sift in the icing sugar and beat together until smooth. When the cakes are cold, spread the icing on top of each cake, then decorate as you like and place a candle in the top of each, if using.

12 *Citrus almond party cakes*

For more grown-up party cakes, replace 55 g/2 oz of the flour with ground almonds and fold in 25 g/1 oz finely chopped mixed peel. Decorate with sugared almonds.

115 g/4 oz plain flour
2 tsp ground ginger
¼ tsp ground cinnamon
1 piece stem ginger, finely chopped
¼ tsp bicarbonate of soda
4 tbsp milk
85 g/3 oz butter, softened
70 g/2½ oz soft dark brown sugar
2 tbsp black treacle

2 eggs, lightly beaten
1 piece stem ginger, sliced,
   to decorate

ICING
85 g/3 oz butter, softened
175 g/6 oz icing sugar
2 tbsp ginger syrup from the stem
   ginger jar

Preheat the oven to 160°C/325°F/ Gas Mark 3. Line two 12-hole bun tins with 16 paper cases. Sift the flour, ground ginger and cinnamon together into a bowl. Add the chopped ginger and toss in the flour mixture until it is well coated. Place the bicarbonate of soda and milk in a separate bowl and stir to dissolve.

Place the butter and sugar in a large bowl and beat together until light and fluffy.

Beat in the black treacle, then gradually mix in the eggs. Beat in the flour mixture and gradually add the milk. Spoon the mixture into the paper cases.

Bake in the preheated oven for 20 minutes, or until well risen and golden brown. Transfer to a wire rack to cool completely.

To make the icing, place the butter in a bowl and beat until fluffy. Sift in the icing sugar, add the ginger syrup and beat together until smooth and creamy.

When the cupcakes are cold, spread the icing on top of each cake, then decorate with pieces of the stem ginger.

21 *Sticky gingersnap cupcakes*

Add 40 g/1½ oz finely chopped walnuts or pecan nuts with the chopped stem ginger. Decorate with chopped nuts.

200 ml/7 fl oz water
85 g/3 oz butter
85 g/3 oz caster sugar
1 tbsp golden syrup
3 tbsp milk
1 tsp vanilla extract
1 tsp bicarbonate of soda
225 g/8 oz plain flour
2 tbsp cocoa powder

TOPPING
50 g/1¾ oz plain chocolate, broken
   into pieces
4 tbsp water
50 g/1¾ oz butter
50 g/1¾ oz white chocolate,
   broken into pieces
350 g/12 oz icing sugar
100 g /3½ oz plain chocolate shavings
and 100 g/3½ oz white chocolate
   shavings, to decorate

Preheat the oven to 180°C/350°F/ Gas Mark 4. Line two 12-hole bun tins with 20 paper cases. Place the water, butter, sugar and syrup in a saucepan and heat gently, stirring, until the sugar has dissolved. Bring to the boil, reduce the heat and cook gently for 5 minutes. Leave to cool.

Meanwhile, place the milk and vanilla extract in a bowl. Add the bicarbonate of soda and stir to dissolve. Sift the flour and cocoa into a separate bowl and add the syrup mixture. Stir in the milk mixture and beat until smooth, then spoon the mixture into the paper cases.

Bake in the preheated oven for 20 minutes, or until well risen and firm to the touch. Transfer to a wire rack to cool completely.

To make the icing, place the plain chocolate in a small heatproof bowl, add half the water and half the butter, set the bowl over a saucepan of gently simmering water and heat until melted. Stir until smooth and then leave to stand over the water. Repeat with the white chocolate and remaining water and butter. Sift half the icing sugar into each bowl and beat until smooth and thick.

When the cupcakes are cold, top alternately with each icing, then leave to set. Decorate with chocolate shavings.

23 *Pecan fudge cupcakes*

Stir 40 g/1½ oz chopped pecan nuts into the flour and cocoa mixture before adding the syrup. Sprinkle chopped nuts instead of chocolate shavings on top of the icing.

. . . .

*55 g/2 oz butter, softened,
or soft margarine
225 g/8 oz soft light brown sugar
115 g/4 oz crunchy peanut butter
2 eggs, lightly beaten
1 tsp vanilla extract
225 g/8 oz plain flour
2 tsp baking powder
100 ml/3½ fl oz milk*

*FROSTING
200 g/7 oz soft cream cheese
25 g/1 oz butter, softened
225 g/8 oz icing sugar*

. . . .

Preheat the oven to 180°C/350°F/
Gas Mark 4. Line two 12-hole bun
tins with 16 paper cases. Place the
butter, sugar and peanut butter
in a bowl and beat together for
1–2 minutes, or until well mixed.
Gradually beat in the eggs, then
add the vanilla extract. Sift in the
flour and baking powder, then fold
them into the mixture, alternating
with the milk. Spoon the mixture
into the paper cases.

Bake in the preheated oven for
25 minutes, or until well risen and
golden brown. Transfer to a wire
rack to cool completely.

To make the frosting, place
the cream cheese and butter in
a large bowl and beat together
until smooth. Sift the icing sugar
into the mixture, beat together
until well mixed, then spread the
frosting on top of each cupcake.

25 *Peanut butter & jam cupcakes*

*Spoon half the mixture into the paper cases then place about ½ teaspoon
of strawberry or raspberry jam into the centre of each. Carefully spoon the
remaining mixture into the paper cases so that it completely encloses the
jam. Sprinkle with a little demerara sugar and bake as before.*

26 *Chocolate peanut butter cupcakes*

*Spoon half the mixture into the paper cases then place about ½ teaspoon
of chocolate spread into the centre of each. Carefully spoon the remaining
mixture into the paper cases so that it completely encloses the chocolate
spread. Bake as before. Cool and spread with extra chocolate spread.*

6 tbsp sunflower oil or 85 g/3 oz butter, melted and cooled, plus extra for greasing
280 g/10 oz plain flour
1 tbsp baking powder
pinch of salt
115 g/4 oz soft light brown sugar

150 g/5½ oz frozen blueberries
2 eggs
250 ml/9 fl oz milk
1 tsp vanilla extract
finely grated rind of 1 lemon

Preheat the oven to 200°C/400°F/Gas Mark 6. Grease a 12-hole muffin tin. Sift together the flour, baking powder and salt into a large bowl. Stir in the sugar and blueberries.

Place the eggs in a large jug or bowl and beat lightly, then beat in the milk, oil, vanilla extract and lemon rind. Make a well in the centre of the dry ingredients and pour in the beaten liquid ingredients. Stir until just combined; do not overmix. Spoon the mixture into the muffin tin.

Bake in the preheated oven for 20 minutes, or until well risen, golden brown and firm to the touch. Leave to cool in the tin for 5 minutes, then serve warm or transfer to a wire rack to cool completely.

28 *With white chocolate topping*

Rub 3 tablespoons of butter into 50 g/1¾ oz plain flour until the mixture resembles breadcrumbs, then stir in 2 tablespoons of caster sugar, 2 tablespoons of dried blueberries and 50 g/1¾ oz grated white chocolate and scatter over the muffins before baking.

29 *Blackberry & apple muffins* MAKES 12

6 tbsp sunflower oil or 85 g/3 oz butter, melted and cooled, plus extra for greasing
280 g/10 oz plain flour
1 tbsp baking powder
pinch of salt
115 g/4 oz soft light brown sugar

1 large apple
2 eggs
250 ml/9 fl oz buttermilk
1 tsp vanilla extract
150 g/5½ oz frozen blackberries
40 g/1½ oz demerara sugar

Preheat the oven to 200°C/400°F/Gas Mark 6. Grease a 12-hole muffin tin. Sift together the flour, baking powder and salt into a large bowl. Stir in the brown sugar. Peel, core and finely chop the apple. Add to the flour mixture and stir together.

Place the eggs in a large jug or bowl and beat lightly, then beat in the buttermilk, oil and vanilla extract. Make a well in the centre of the dry ingredients, pour in the beaten liquid ingredients and add the blackberries. Stir gently until just combined; do not overmix. Spoon the mixture into the muffin tin. Sprinkle the demerara sugar over the tops of the muffins.

Bake in the preheated oven for 20 minutes, until well risen, golden brown and firm to the touch. Leave to cool in the tin for 5 minutes, then serve warm or transfer to a wire rack to cool completely.

30 *Mixed berry muffins*

Omit the apple and replace the blackberries with 200 g/7 oz mixed fresh berries.

280 g/10 oz plain flour
1 tbsp baking powder
½ tsp ground cinnamon
pinch of salt
115 g/4 oz soft light brown sugar
1 large apple
2 eggs
250 ml/9 fl oz milk

6 tbsp sunflower oil or 85 g/3 oz butter, melted and cooled

STREUSEL TOPPING
50 g/1¾ oz plain flour
¼ tsp ground cinnamon
35 g/1¼ oz butter, cut into small pieces
2 tbsp soft light brown sugar

Preheat the oven to 200°C/400°F/Gas Mark 6. Line a 12-hole muffin tin with 12 paper cases.

To make the streusel topping, place the flour and cinnamon in a bowl. Add the butter and rub it in with your fingertips until the mixture resembles fine breadcrumbs. Stir in the sugar and set aside.

To make the muffins, sift together the flour, baking powder, cinnamon and salt into a large bowl. Stir in the sugar. Peel, core and finely chop the apple. Add to the flour mixture and stir together. Place the eggs in a large jug or bowl and beat lightly, then beat in the milk and oil.

Make a well in the centre of the dry ingredients and pour in the beaten liquid ingredients. Stir gently until just combined; do not overmix. Spoon the mixture into the paper cases. Scatter the streusel topping over each muffin.

Bake in the preheated oven for 20 minutes, or until well risen, golden brown and firm to the touch. Leave to cool in the tin for 5 minutes, then serve warm or transfer to a wire rack to cool completely.

32 *With apple brandy butter*

Beat 1 tablespoon of apple brandy and 2 tablespoons of finely chopped dried apple into 6 tablespoons of softened butter and serve with the muffins.

6 tbsp sunflower oil or 85 g/3 oz butter, melted and cooled, plus extra for greasing
280 g/10 oz plain flour
1 tbsp baking powder
pinch of salt

115 g/4 oz caster sugar
55 g/2 oz dried apricots, finely chopped
2 bananas
about 150 ml/5 fl oz milk
2 eggs

Preheat the oven to 200°C/400°F/Gas Mark 6. Grease a 12-hole muffin tin. Sift together the flour, baking powder and salt into a large bowl. Stir in the sugar and apricots.

Mash the bananas and place in a jug, then add enough milk to make up the purée to a 250 ml/9 fl oz.

Place the eggs in a large jug or bowl and beat lightly, then beat in the banana and milk mixture and the oil. Make a well in the centre of the dry ingredients and pour in the beaten liquid ingredients. Stir until just combined; do not overmix. Spoon the mixture into the muffin tin.

Bake in the preheated oven for 20 minutes, or until well risen, golden brown and firm to the touch. Leave to cool in the tin for 5 minutes, then serve warm or transfer to a wire rack to cool completely.

Walnut & cinnamon muffins

280 g/10 oz plain flour
1 tbsp baking powder
1 tsp ground cinnamon
pinch of salt
115 g/4 oz soft light brown sugar
100 g/3½ oz walnuts, coarsely chopped

2 eggs
250 ml/9 fl oz milk
6 tbsp sunflower oil or 85 g/3 oz butter, melted and cooled
1 tsp vanilla extract

Preheat the oven to 200°C/400°F/Gas Mark 6. Line a 12-hole muffin tin with 12 paper cases. Sift together the flour, baking powder, cinnamon and salt into a large bowl. Stir in the sugar and walnuts.

Place the eggs in a large jug or bowl and beat lightly, then beat in the milk, oil and vanilla extract. Make a well in the centre of the dry ingredients and pour in the beaten liquid ingredients. Stir gently until just combined; do not overmix. Spoon the mixture into the paper cases.

Bake in the preheated oven for 20 minutes, or until well risen, golden brown and firm to the touch. Leave to cool in the tin for 5 minutes, then serve warm or transfer to a wire rack to cool completely.

35 *Hazelnut & vanilla seed muffins*

Replace the walnuts and cinnamon with 100 g/3½ oz chopped toasted hazelnuts and the seeds from a vanilla pod.

36 *Lemon & poppy seed muffins*

350 g/12 oz plain flour
1 tbsp baking powder
115 g/4 oz caster sugar
2 tbsp poppy seeds

4 tbsp butter
1 egg, lightly beaten
225 ml/8 fl oz milk
finely grated rind and juice of 1 lemon

Preheat the oven to 190°C/375°F/Gas Mark 5. Line a 12-hole muffin tin with 12 paper cases. Sift the flour and baking powder into a large bowl and stir in the sugar.

Heat a heavy-based frying pan over a medium–high heat and add the poppy seeds, then toast for about 30 seconds, shaking the frying pan to prevent them burning. Remove from the heat and add to the flour mixture.

Place the butter in a saucepan and heat over a low heat until melted. Transfer to a bowl and beat with the egg, milk, lemon rind and juice. Pour into the dry mixture and stir well to form a soft, sticky dough. Add a little more milk if it is too dry. Spoon the mixture into the paper cases.

Bake in the preheated oven for 25–30 minutes, or until risen, golden brown and firm to touch. Transfer to a wire rack to cool completely.

6 tbsp sunflower oil or 85 g/3 oz
  butter, melted and cooled, plus extra
  for greasing
280 g/10 oz plain flour
1 tbsp baking powder
1 tsp ground cinnamon
½ tsp ground allspice
½ tsp freshly grated nutmeg
pinch of salt
115 g/4 oz soft light brown sugar
2 eggs
250 ml/9 fl oz double cream
icing sugar, for dusting

Preheat the oven to 200°C/400°F/Gas Mark 6. Grease a 12-hole muffin tin. Sift together the flour, baking powder, cinnamon, allspice, nutmeg and salt into a large bowl. Stir in the brown sugar.

Place the eggs in a large jug or bowl and beat lightly, then beat in the cream and oil. Make a well in the centre of the dry ingredients and pour in the beaten liquid ingredients. Stir gently until just combined; do not overmix. Spoon the mixture into the muffin tin.

Bake in the preheated oven for 20 minutes, or until well risen, golden brown and firm to the touch. Leave to cool in the tin for 5 minutes, then serve warm or transfer to a wire rack to cool completely. Dust with sifted icing sugar before serving.

38 *With spice butter topping*

Blend 150 g/5½ oz butter with 3 tablespoons of icing sugar and 1 teaspoon of mixed spice, then spread over the cooled muffins.

250 g/9 oz plain flour
25 g/1 oz cocoa powder
2 tsp baking powder
½ tsp bicarbonate of soda
100 g/3½ oz plain chocolate chips
100 g/3½ oz white chocolate chips
85 g/3 oz soft light brown sugar
2 eggs, lightly beaten
300 ml/10 fl oz soured cream
85 g/3 oz butter, melted

Preheat the oven to 200°C/400°F/Gas Mark 6. Line a 12-hole muffin tin with 12 paper cases. Sift the flour, cocoa, baking powder and bicarbonate of soda into a large bowl, then stir in the plain and white chocolate chips. Stir in the sugar.

Place the eggs, soured cream and butter in a separate bowl and mix well. Add the wet ingredients to the dry ingredients and stir gently until just combined. Spoon the mixture into the paper cases.

Bake in the preheated oven for 20 minutes, or until well risen and firm to the touch. Leave to cool in the tin for 5 minutes, then serve warm or transfer to a wire rack to cool completely.

40 *Chocolate & cherry muffins*

Replace the white chocolate chips with 85 g/3 oz chopped glacé cherries.

41 Oat & cranberry muffins

6 tbsp sunflower oil, plus extra
   for greasing
140 g/5 oz plain flour
1 tbsp baking powder
115 g/4 oz soft dark brown sugar
140 g/5 oz porridge oats

85 g/3 oz dried cranberries
2 eggs
250 ml/9 fl oz buttermilk
1 tsp vanilla extract

Preheat the oven to 200°C/400°F/Gas Mark 6. Grease a 12-hole muffin tin. Sift together the flour and baking powder into a large bowl. Stir in the sugar, oats and cranberries.

Place the eggs in a large jug or bowl and beat lightly, then beat in the buttermilk, oil and vanilla extract. Make a well in the centre of the dry ingredients and pour in the beaten liquid ingredients. Stir gently until just combined; do not overmix. Spoon the mixture into the muffin tin.

Bake in the preheated oven for 20 minutes, or until well risen, golden brown and firm to the touch. Leave to cool in the tin for 5 minutes, then serve warm or transfer to a wire rack to cool completely.

42 Fresh cranberry oat-topped muffins

Omit the dried cranberries and replace with 125 g/4½ oz fresh cranberries. Scatter 3 tablespoons of porridge oats over the muffins before baking.

43 Raisin bran muffins

6 tbsp sunflower oil, plus extra
   for greasing
140 g/5 oz plain flour
1 tbsp baking powder
140 g/5 oz wheat bran
115 g/4 oz caster sugar

165 g/5¾ oz raisins
2 eggs
250 ml/9 fl oz skimmed milk
1 tsp vanilla extract

Preheat the oven to 200°C/400°F/Gas Mark 6. Grease a 12-hole muffin tin. Sift together the flour and baking powder into a large bowl. Stir in the bran, sugar and raisins.

Place the eggs in a large jug or bowl and beat lightly, then beat in the milk, oil and vanilla extract. Make a well in the centre of the dry ingredients and pour in the beaten liquid ingredients. Stir gently until just combined; do not overmix. Spoon the mixture into the muffin tin.

Bake in the preheated oven for 20 minutes, or until well risen, golden brown and firm to the touch. Leave to cool in the tin for 5 minutes, then serve warm or transfer to a wire rack to cool completely.

Healthy oat & prune muffins

140 g/5 oz plain flour
1 tbsp baking powder
115 g/4 oz soft light brown sugar
140 g/5 oz porridge oats
150 g/5½ oz stoned prunes, chopped

2 eggs
250 ml/9 fl oz buttermilk
6 tbsp sunflower oil
1 tsp vanilla extract

Preheat the oven to 200°C/400°F/Gas Mark 6. Line a 12-hole muffin tin with 12 paper cases. Sift together the flour and baking powder into a large bowl. Stir in the sugar, oats and prunes.

Place the eggs in a large jug or bowl and beat lightly, then beat in the buttermilk, oil and vanilla extract. Make a well in the centre of the dry ingredients and pour in the beaten liquid ingredients. Stir gently until just combined; do not overmix. Spoon the mixture into the paper cases.

Bake in the preheated oven for 20 minutes, or until well risen, golden brown and firm to the touch. Leave to cool in the tin for 5 minutes, then serve warm or transfer to a wire rack to cool completely.

45 Apricot & sunflower seed muffins

Omit the prunes and replace with 150 g/5½ oz chopped soft dried apricots and scatter over 3 tablespoons of sunflower seeds before baking the muffins.

46 Granola muffins

6 tbsp sunflower oil, plus extra
    for greasing
40 g/1½ oz wholemeal flour
140 g/5 oz plain flour
1 tbsp baking powder
85 g/3 oz soft light brown sugar
2 eggs
250 ml/9 fl oz skimmed milk

GRANOLA
75 g/2¾ oz porridge oats
25 g/1 oz blanched almonds, chopped
scant 2 tbsp sunflower seeds
25 g/1 oz raisins
2 tbsp soft light brown sugar

Preheat the oven to 200°C/400°F/Gas Mark 6. Grease a 12-hole muffin tin. Sift together both flours and the baking powder into a large bowl, adding any bran left in the sieve. Stir in the sugar and granola.

Place the eggs in a large jug or bowl and beat lightly, then beat in the milk and oil. Make a well in the centre of the dry ingredients and pour in the beaten liquid ingredients. Stir gently until just combined; do not overmix. Spoon the mixture into the muffin tin.

Bake in the preheated oven for 20 minutes, or until well risen, golden brown and firm to the touch. Leave to cool in the tin for 5 minutes, then serve warm or transfer to a wire rack to cool completely.

To make the granola, place the oats in a large, dry frying pan and toast over a low heat for 1 minute. Add the almonds, sunflower seeds and raisins and toast for 6–8 minutes, or until browned. Add the sugar and stir for 1 minute until it melts. Remove from the heat and stir until mixed.

47 Apricot & pecan muffins

Omit the raisins from the granola, add 55 g/2 oz chopped dried apricots, and replace the almonds with 30 g/1 oz chopped pecan nuts.

85 g/3 oz butter, softened,
or soft margarine
100 g/3½ oz caster sugar
1 egg, lightly beaten
85 g/3 oz self-raising flour
25 g/1 oz ground almonds
grated rind and juice of
1 small orange

TOPPING
1 orange
55 g/2 oz caster sugar
1 tbsp toasted flaked almonds

Preheat the oven to 180°C/350°F/ Gas Mark 4. Line a 12-hole muffin tin with 12 paper cases. Place the butter and sugar in a large bowl and beat together until light and fluffy, then gradually beat in the egg. Add the flour, ground almonds and orange rind and fold into the mixture, then fold in the orange juice. Spoon the mixture into the paper cases.

Bake in the preheated oven for 20–25 minutes, or until well risen and golden brown.

Meanwhile, make the topping. Using a citrus zester, pare the rind from the orange, then squeeze the juice. Place the rind, juice and sugar in a saucepan and heat gently, stirring, until the sugar has dissolved, then leave to simmer for 5 minutes.

When the cupcakes are cooked, prick them all over with a skewer and spoon the warm syrup and rind over each cake.

Scatter the flaked almonds on top and transfer to a wire rack to cool completely.

49 *Shredded lemon cupcakes*

Replace the orange rind and juice with lemon rind and juice.

50 *Lime & coconut cupcakes*

Replace the orange rind and juice in the cake with the rind and juice of 1½ limes. Add 25 g/1 oz desiccated coconut to the mixture. For the topping, use the pared rind of 1 lime and the juice of 2 limes in place of the orange. Replace the almonds with toasted desiccated coconut.

51 *Mocha cupcakes with whipped cream* MAKES 20

2 tbsp instant espresso coffee powder
85 g/3 oz butter
100 g/3½ oz caster sugar
1 tbsp honey
200 ml/7 fl oz water
225 g/8 oz plain flour
2 tbsp cocoa powder
1 tsp bicarbonate of soda
3 tbsp milk
1 egg, lightly beaten

TOPPING
225 ml/8 fl oz whipping cream
cocoa powder, for dusting

Preheat the oven to 180°C/350°F/ Gas Mark 4. Line two 12-hole muffin tins with 20 paper cases. Place the coffee powder, butter, sugar, honey and water in a saucepan and heat gently, stirring, until the sugar has dissolved. Bring to the boil, then reduce the heat and leave to simmer for 5 minutes. Pour into a large heatproof bowl and leave to cool. When the mixture has cooled, sift in the flour and cocoa. Place the bicarbonate of soda and milk in a bowl and stir to dissolve, then add to the mixture with the egg and beat together until smooth. Spoon the mixture into the paper cases.

Bake in the preheated oven for 15–20 minutes, or until well risen and firm to the touch. Transfer to a wire rack to cool completely.

For the topping, place the cream in a bowl and whip until it holds its shape. Spoon heaped teaspoonfuls of cream on top of each cake, then dust lightly with sifted cocoa.

52 *Mocha walnut cupcakes*

Add 40 g/1½ oz chopped walnuts to the mixture. For the topping, dissolve 2 teaspoons of coffee powder in 1 tablespoon of boiling water and leave to cool. Lightly whip the cream until it begins to hold its shape, then add the coffee and 2 tablespoons of icing sugar and whip until soft peaks form. Spread on the cakes and decorate with walnut halves.

400 g/14 oz canned peach slices
in fruit juice
115 g/4 oz butter, softened
115 g/4 oz caster sugar
2 eggs, lightly beaten
115 g/4 oz self-raising flour
150 ml/5 fl oz double cream

Preheat the oven to 180°C/350°F/ Gas Mark 4. Line a 12-hole muffin tin with 12 paper cases. Drain the peaches, reserving the juice. Set aside 12 small slices and finely chop the remaining slices.

Place the butter and sugar in a large bowl and beat together until light and fluffy. Gradually beat in the eggs. Sift in the flour and fold into the mixture. Fold in the chopped peaches and 1 tablespoon of the reserved juice. Spoon the mixture into the paper cases.

Bake in the oven for 25 minutes, or until golden brown. Leave the cupcakes to cool in the tin for 10 minutes, then transfer to a wire rack to cool completely.

When ready to decorate, place the cream in a bowl and whip until soft peaks form. Spread the cream on top of the cupcakes, using a knife to form the cream into peaks. Place the reserved peach slices on top to decorate.

54 *Apricot cream cupcakes*

Use 8 apricot halves in fruit juice instead of the peach slices. Slice 4 halves into 3 slices each and set aside for decoration. Finely chop the 4 remaining apricot halves and add to the mix with 1 tablespoon of juice from the can.

55 *Dried apricot cupcakes*

Replace the can of peach slices with 85 g/3 oz finely chopped ready-to-eat dried apricots and add 1 tablespoon of orange juice to replace the fruit juice from the can. To decorate, dust lightly with sifted icing sugar.

56 Moist walnut cupcakes

85 g/3 oz walnuts
55 g/2 oz butter, softened, cut into
small pieces
100 g/3½ oz caster sugar
grated rind of ½ lemon
70 g/2½ oz self-raising flour
2 eggs
12 walnut halves, to decorate

ICING
55 g/2 oz butter, softened
85 g/3 oz icing sugar
grated rind of ½ lemon
1 tsp lemon juice

Preheat the oven to 190°C/375°F/ Gas Mark 5. Line a 12-hole muffin tin with 12 paper cases. Place the walnuts in a food processor and pulse until finely ground. Be careful not to overgrind, or the nuts will turn to oil.

Add the butter, sugar, lemon rind, flour and eggs and blend until the mixture is evenly combined. Spoon the mixture into the paper cases.

Bake in the preheated oven for 20 minutes, or until well risen and golden brown. Transfer to a wire rack to cool completely.

To make the icing, place the butter in a bowl and beat until fluffy. Sift in the icing sugar, add the lemon rind and juice and mix well together. When the cupcakes are cold, spread the icing on top of each cupcake and top with a walnut to decorate.

57 Sticky orange & walnut cupcakes

For the cupcakes, replace the lemon rind with orange rind. Instead of the icing, heat 6 tablespoons of orange juice with 2 tablespoons of caster sugar, stirring until the sugar dissolves, then boil until syrupy. Spoon the syrup over the hot cakes and leave to cool before serving.

58 Moist pecan cupcakes

Replace the walnuts with pecan nuts and the lemon rind and juice with orange rind and juice.

59 Feathered-iced coffee cupcakes

1 tbsp instant coffee granules
1 tbsp boiling water
115 g/4 oz butter, softened,
or soft margarine
100 g/3½ oz soft light brown sugar
2 eggs
100 g/3½ oz self-raising flour
½ tsp baking powder
2 tbsp soured cream

ICING
225 g/8 oz icing sugar
4 tsp warm water
1 tsp instant coffee granules
2 tsp boiling water

Preheat the oven to 190°C/375°F/ Gas Mark 5. Line two 12-hole muffin tins with 16 paper cases. Place the coffee granules in a cup or small bowl, add the boiling water and stir until dissolved.

Cool slightly. Place the butter, sugar and eggs in a large bowl. Sift in the flour and baking powder and beat until smooth. Add the dissolved coffee and soured cream and beat until mixed. Spoon the mixture into the paper cases.

Bake in the preheated oven for 20 minutes, or until well risen and golden. Cool on a wire rack.

To make the icing, sift 90 g/ 3¼ oz of the icing sugar into a bowl and add enough warm water to mix until thick enough to coat the back of a wooden spoon. Dissolve the coffee in the boiling water. Sift the remaining icing sugar into a bowl and stir in the dissolved coffee. Ice the cakes with the white icing, then pipe the coffee icing in parallel lines on top. Draw a skewer across the piped lines in both directions. Leave to set.

60 Feathered-iced mocha cupcakes

Replace the soured cream with 55 g/2 oz melted plain chocolate.

61 Feathered-iced chocolate cupcakes

Replace the coffee granules for the cake mixture with cocoa powder. To complete the cakes, melt 175 g/6 oz milk chocolate and 25 g/1 oz white chocolate in separate bowls and spoon the white chocolate into a piping bag fitted with a piping nozzle. Spread the milk chocolate over the top of the cakes, then quickly pipe the white chocolate in lines across the cakes. Drag a skewer across the piped lines in both directions to feather the chocolate.

62 Queen cakes

115 g/4 oz butter, softened, or soft
margarine
100 g/3½ oz caster sugar
2 eggs, lightly beaten
4 tsp lemon juice
175 g/6 oz self-raising flour
125 g/4½ oz raisins
2–4 tbsp milk, if necessary

Preheat the oven to 190°C/375°F/Gas Mark 5. Line two 12-hole muffin tins with 18 paper cases. Place the butter and sugar in a large bowl and beat together until light and fluffy. Gradually beat in the eggs, then beat in the lemon juice with 1 tablespoon of the flour. Fold in the remaining flour and the raisins. If necessary, add a little milk to create a soft dropping consistency. Spoon the mixture into the paper cases.

Bake in the preheated oven for 15–20 minutes, or until well risen and golden brown. Transfer to a wire rack to cool completely.

63 Orange queen cakes

Replace the lemon juice with orange juice and add the grated rind of ½ orange with the juice.

64 Iced queen cakes

Sift 125 g/4½ oz icing sugar into a small bowl and stir in about 4 teaspoons of lemon juice. Mix to a smooth icing that coats the back of a wooden spoon. Spread the icing over the cakes almost to the edges.

65 Carrot & orange cupcakes

115 g/4 oz butter, softened,
or soft margarine
115 g/4 oz soft light brown sugar
juice and finely grated rind
of 1 small orange
2 eggs, lightly beaten
175 g/6 oz carrots, grated
25 g/1 oz walnut pieces,
roughly chopped
140 g/5 oz plain flour
1 tsp mixed spice
1½ tsp baking powder

FROSTING
300 g/10 oz mascarpone cheese
4 tbsp icing sugar
grated rind of 1 large orange

Preheat the oven to 180°C/350°F/Gas Mark 4. Line a 12-hole muffin tin with 12 paper cases.

Place the butter, sugar and orange rind in a bowl and beat together until light and fluffy, then gradually beat in the eggs. Squeeze any excess liquid from the carrots and add to the mixture with the walnuts and orange juice. Stir until well mixed. Sift in the flour, mixed spice and baking powder and fold in. Spoon the mixture into the paper cases.

Bake in the preheated oven for 25 minutes, or until risen, firm to the touch and golden brown. Transfer to a wire rack to cool completely.

To make the frosting, place the mascarpone cheese, icing sugar and orange rind in a large bowl and beat together until they are well mixed.

When the cupcakes are cold, spread the frosting on top of each cupcake, swirling it with a round-bladed knife.

66 Carrot & lemon cupcakes

Replace the orange rind and juice in the cakes with lemon rind and juice. Instead of the frosting, sift 175 g/6 oz icing sugar into a large bowl and beat in enough lemon juice to make a smooth icing. Spread on top of the cakes and leave plain or decorate with lemon candy slices.

67 Chocolate carrot cupcakes

Add 85 g/3 oz plain chocolate chips along with the carrot. Beat 55 g/2 oz melted plain chocolate into the mascarpone frosting before spreading on the cupcakes.

85 g/3 oz butter, softened,
or soft margarine
100 g/3½ oz caster sugar
2 eggs, lightly beaten
2 tbsp milk
55 g/2 oz plain chocolate chips
225 g/8 oz self-raising flour
25 g/1 oz cocoa powder

TOPPING
225 g/8 oz white chocolate,
broken into pieces
150 g/5½ oz low-fat cream cheese
chocolate curls, to decorate

Preheat the oven to 200°C/400°F/ Gas Mark 6. Line two 12-hole muffin tins with 18 paper cases.

Place the butter and sugar in a large bowl and beat together until light and fluffy, then gradually beat in the eggs. Add the milk, then fold in the chocolate chips. Sift in the flour and cocoa, then fold into the mixture. Spoon the mixture into the paper cases and smooth the tops.

Bake in the preheated oven for 20 minutes, or until well risen and springy to the touch. Transfer to a wire rack to cool completely.

To make the frosting, place the chocolate in a small heatproof bowl, set the bowl over a saucepan of gently simmering water, and heat until melted. Leave to cool slightly. Place the cream cheese in a separate bowl and beat until softened, then beat in the slightly cooled chocolate.

When the cupcakes are cold, spread a little of the frosting over the top of each cupcake, then leave to chill in the refrigerator for 1 hour before serving. Decorate with a few chocolate curls, if liked.

69 *White chocolate cupcakes*

Replace the plain chocolate chips with 70 g/2½ oz white chocolate chips. Omit the cocoa and increase the flour to 250 g/9 oz. Decorate with white chocolate curls made with a vegetable peeler.

70 *With chocolate mascarpone frosting*

For the frosting, replace the cream cheese with mascarpone and decorate with milk chocolate curls.

---

71 *Lemon butterfly cakes* MAKES 12

115 g/4 oz self-raising flour
½ tsp baking powder
115 g/4 oz butter, softened
115 g/4 oz caster sugar
2 eggs
finely grated rind of ½ lemon
2 tbsp milk
icing sugar, for dusting

LEMON BUTTERCREAM
85 g/3 oz butter, softened
175 g/6 oz icing sugar
1 tbsp lemon juice

Preheat the oven to 190°C/375°F/ Gas Mark 5. Line a 12-hole muffin tin with 12 paper cases.

Sift the flour and baking powder into a large bowl, add the butter, sugar, eggs, lemon rind and milk, and beat together until smooth. Spoon the mixture into the paper cases.

Bake in the preheated oven for 15–20 minutes, or until well risen and golden brown. Transfer to a wire rack to cool completely.

To make the buttercream, place the butter in a bowl and beat until fluffy. Sift in the icing sugar, add the lemon juice and beat together until smooth and creamy. When the cupcakes are cold, cut the top off each cake then cut the top in half.

Spread or pipe a little of the lemon buttercream over the cut surface of each cupcake, then gently press the 2 cut cake pieces into it at an angle to resemble butterfly wings. Dust with sifted icing sugar before serving.

72 *Orange butterfly cakes*

Replace the lemon rind and juice with orange rind and juice.

73 *Vanilla butterfly cakes*

Omit the lemon rind from the cake mixture and replace the lemon juice in the buttercream with 1 teaspoon of vanilla extract. Decorate with sugar sprinkles, if liked.

½ tsp bicarbonate of soda
280 g/10 oz jar apple sauce
55 g/2 oz butter, softened,
or soft margarine
100 g/3½ oz demerara sugar
1 egg, lightly beaten
175 g/6 oz self-raising flour
½ tsp ground cinnamon
½ tsp freshly ground nutmeg

TOPPING
50 g/1¾ oz plain flour
55 g/2 oz demerara sugar
¼ tsp ground cinnamon
¼ tsp freshly grated nutmeg
50 g/1¾ oz butter,
cut into small pieces

Preheat the oven to 180°C/350°F/
Gas Mark 4. Line two 12-hole
muffin tins with 14 paper cases.

First, make the topping. Place
the flour, sugar, cinnamon and
nutmeg in a large bowl. Add the
butter and rub it in with your
fingertips until the mixture
resembles fine breadcrumbs.
Set aside until required.

To make the cupcakes, add
the bicarbonate of soda to the
jar of apple sauce and stir until
dissolved. Place the butter and
sugar in a large bowl and beat
together until light and fluffy,
then gradually beat in the egg.
Sift in the flour, cinnamon
and nutmeg and fold into the

mixture, alternating with the
apple sauce. Spoon the mixture
into the paper cases. Scatter
the reserved topping over each

cupcake to cover the tops and
press down gently. Bake in the
preheated oven for 20 minutes, or
until well risen and golden brown.

Leave the cakes for 2–3 minutes
in the tins before serving warm,
or transfer to a wire rack to cool
completely.

75 *Apricot streusel cupcakes*

*Drain 280 g/10 oz canned apricots, reserving the juice. Chop the apricots
and mix a little of the juice with 1 teaspoon of cornflour. Place the apricots in
a saucepan with the juice and bring to the boil. Add the cornflour mixture,
and cook over a low heat, stirring, until thickened. Leave to cool, then
complete as before, replacing the apple sauce with the apricot mixture.*

76 *Cranberry streusel cupcakes*

Replace the apple sauce with cranberry sauce.

77 *Cherry streusel cupcakes*

Replace the apple sauce with 200 g/7 oz canned cherry pie filling.

6 tbsp sunflower oil or 85 g/3 oz butter, melted and cooled, plus extra for greasing
280 g/10 oz plain flour
1 tbsp baking powder
½ tsp bicarbonate of soda
pinch of salt
115 g/4 oz caster sugar
2 eggs

250 ml/9 fl oz natural yogurt
1 tsp vanilla extract
150 g/5½ oz frozen raspberries

CRUMBLE TOPPING
50 g/1¾ oz plain flour
35 g/1¼ oz butter, cut into pieces
2 tbsp caster sugar

Preheat the oven to 200°C/400°F/ Gas Mark 6. Grease a 12-hole muffin tin.

To make the crumble topping, place the flour into a bowl. Add the butter and rub it in with your fingertips until the mixture resembles fine breadcrumbs. Stir in the sugar and set aside.

To make the muffins, sift together the flour, baking powder, bicarbonate of soda and salt into a large bowl. Stir in the sugar. Place the eggs in a large jug or bowl and beat lightly, then beat in the yogurt, oil and vanilla extract. Make a well in the centre of the dry ingredients, pour in the beaten liquid ingredients and add the raspberries.

Stir gently until just combined; do not overmix. Spoon the mixture into the muffin tin. Scatter the crumble topping over each muffin and then press down lightly.

Bake in the preheated oven for 20 minutes, or until well risen, golden brown, and firm to the touch. Leave to cool in the tin for 5 minutes, then serve warm or transfer to a wire rack to cool completely.

79 *With almond crunch topping*

Add 50 g/1¾ oz chopped toasted flaked almonds and 6 crushed amaretti biscuits to the crumble topping before scattering over the muffins.

80 *Soured cream & pineapple muffins*

6 tbsp sunflower oil or 85 g/3 oz butter, melted and cooled, plus extra for greasing
2 canned pineapple slices in natural juice, plus 2 tbsp juice from the can
280 g/10 oz plain flour
1 tbsp baking powder
pinch of salt
115 g/4 oz caster sugar
2 eggs
200 ml/7 fl oz soured cream
1 tsp vanilla extract

Preheat the oven to 200°C/400°F/Gas Mark 6. Grease a 12-hole muffin tin. Drain and finely chop the pineapple slices.

Sift together the flour, baking powder and salt into a large bowl. Stir in the sugar and chopped pineapple.

Place the eggs in a large jug or bowl and beat lightly, then beat in the soured cream, oil, pineapple juice and vanilla extract. Make a well in the centre of the dry ingredients and pour in the beaten liquid ingredients. Stir gently until just combined; do not overmix. Spoon the mixture into the muffin tin.

Bake in the preheated oven for 20 minutes, or until well risen, golden brown and firm to the touch. Leave to cool in the tin for 5 minutes, then serve warm or transfer to a wire rack to cool completely.

81 *With pineapple frosting*

Beat 100 g/3½ oz cream cheese with 2 tablespoons of icing sugar and 1 tablespoon of pineapple juice, then spread over the cooled muffins.

Spicy apple & oat muffins

6 tbsp sunflower oil, plus extra
    for greasing
140 g/5 oz plain flour
1 tbsp baking powder
1 tsp mixed spice
115 g/4 oz soft light brown sugar

175 g/6 oz porridge oats
1 large apple
2 eggs
125 ml/4 fl oz skimmed milk
125 ml/4 fl oz fresh apple juice

Preheat the oven to 200°C/400°F/Gas Mark 6. Grease a 12-hole muffin tin. Sift together the flour, baking powder and mixed spice into a large bowl. Stir in the sugar and 140 g/5 oz of the oats.

Finely chop the unpeeled apple, discarding the core. Add to the flour mixture and stir together.

Place the eggs in a large jug or bowl and beat lightly, then beat in the milk, apple juice and oil. Make a well in the centre of the dry ingredients and pour in the beaten liquid ingredients. Stir gently until just combined; do not overmix. Spoon the mixture into the muffin tin and sprinkle the tops with the remaining oats.

Bake in the preheated oven for 20 minutes, or until well risen, golden brown and firm to the touch. Leave to cool in the tin for 5 minutes, then serve warm or transfer to a wire rack to cool completely.

83 ## Pear, oat & nutmeg muffins

Replace the apple and apple juice with 2 medium peeled, cored and chopped pears and pear juice, and add ½ teaspoon of ground nutmeg.

Spicy dried fruit muffins

6 tbsp sunflower oil or 85 g/3 oz butter,
    melted and cooled
280 g/10 oz plain flour
1 tbsp baking powder
1 tbsp mixed spice
pinch of salt

115 g/4 oz caster sugar
175 g/6 oz mixed dried fruit
2 eggs
250 ml/9 fl oz milk

Preheat the oven to 200°C/400°F/Gas Mark 6. Line a 12-hole muffin tin with 12 paper cases. Sift together the flour, baking powder, mixed spice and salt into a large bowl. Stir in the sugar and dried fruit.

Place the eggs in a large jug or bowl and beat lightly, then beat in the milk and oil. Make a well in the centre of the dry ingredients and pour in the beaten liquid ingredients. Stir gently until just combined; do not overmix. Spoon the mixture into the paper cases.

Bake in the preheated oven for 20 minutes, or until well risen, golden brown and firm to the touch. Leave to cool in the tin for 5 minutes, then serve warm or transfer to a wire rack to cool completely.

85 ## With brandy cream

Whip 200 ml/7 fl oz double cream with 1 tablespoon of brandy and 1 tablespoon of caster sugar until stiff, then spoon onto the cooled muffins.

Apple & cinnamon muffins

200 g/7 oz wholemeal flour
70 g/2¼ oz fine oatmeal
2 tsp baking powder
125 g/4½ oz soft light brown sugar
2 eggs

225 ml/8 fl oz semi-skimmed milk
100 ml/3½ fl oz groundnut oil
1 tsp vanilla extract
1 tsp ground cinnamon
1 large cooking apple

Preheat the oven to 180°C/350°F/Gas Mark 4. Line a 12-hole muffin tin with paper cases.

Sift the flour, oatmeal and baking powder together into a large bowl, then add the larger particles left in the sieve. Stir in the sugar. Place the eggs, milk and oil in a separate bowl and beat together until well combined. Add to the dry ingredients, along with the vanilla extract and cinnamon, and stir until just combined; do not overmix.

Peel, core and grate the apple and stir into the mixture, then spoon the mixture into the paper cases.

Bake in the preheated oven for 20–25 minutes, or until risen and golden brown. Leave to cool in the tin for a few minutes before serving warm or transfer to a wire rack to cool completely.

Buttermilk berry muffins

6 tbsp sunflower oil or 85 g/3 oz
butter, melted and cooled, plus
extra for greasing
150 g/5½ oz frozen mixed berries,
such as blueberries, raspberries,
blackberries, strawberries
280 g/10 oz plain flour
1 tbsp baking powder
pinch of salt
115 g/4 oz caster sugar
2 eggs
250 ml/9 fl oz buttermilk
1 tsp vanilla extract
icing sugar, for dusting

Preheat the oven to 200°C/400°F/ Gas Mark 6. Grease a 12-hole muffin tin. Cut any large berries, such as strawberries, into small pieces. Sift together the flour, baking powder and salt into a large bowl. Stir in the sugar.

Place the eggs in a large jug or bowl and beat lightly, then beat in the buttermilk, oil and vanilla extract. Make a well in the centre of the dry ingredients, pour in the beaten liquid ingredients and add the berries. Stir until combined; do not overmix. Spoon the mixture into the muffin tin.

Bake in the preheated oven for 20 minutes, or until well risen, golden brown and firm to the touch. Leave to cool in the tin for 5 minutes, then serve warm or transfer to a wire rack to cool completely. Dust with a little sifted icing sugar before serving.

88 ## Buttermilk cranberry muffins

Replace the frozen berries with 150 g/5½ oz frozen cranberries mixed with ½ teaspoon of finely grated orange rind.

89 *Iced chocolate orange muffins*

MAKES 12

6 tbsp sunflower oil or 85 g/3 oz butter,
    melted and cooled, plus extra
    for greasing
2 oranges
about 125 ml/4 fl oz milk
225 g/8 oz plain flour
55 g/2 oz cocoa powder
1 tbsp baking powder
pinch of salt
115 g/4 oz soft light brown sugar

140 g/5 oz plain chocolate chips
2 eggs
strips of orange zest, to decorate

ICING
55 g/2 oz plain chocolate, broken into
    pieces
2 tbsp butter
2 tbsp water
175 g/6 oz icing sugar

Preheat the oven to 200°C/400°F/ Gas Mark 6. Grease a 12-hole muffin tin. Finely grate the rind from the oranges and squeeze the juice. Add enough milk to make up the juice to 250 ml/9 fl oz, then add the orange rind. Sift together the flour, cocoa baking powder and salt into a large bowl. Stir in the sugar and chocolate chips.

Place the eggs in a large jug or bowl and beat lightly, then beat in the milk and orange mixture and the oil. Make a well in the centre of the dry ingredients and pour in the beaten liquid ingredients. Stir gently until just combined; do not overmix. Spoon the mixture into the muffin tin.

Bake in the preheated oven for 20 minutes, or until well risen and firm to the touch. Leave to cool in the tin for 5 minutes, then transfer to a wire rack to cool completely.

To make the icing, place the chocolate in a heatproof bowl, add the butter and water, then set the bowl over a saucepan of gently simmering water and heat, stirring, until melted. Remove from the heat, sift in the icing sugar, and beat until smooth, then spread the icing on top of the muffins and decorate with strips of orange zest.

90 *With white chocolate icing*

Replace the plain chocolate with 55 g/2 oz white chocolate and top the muffins with crushed orange-flavoured chocolate.

91 *Brandied peach muffins*

MAKES 12

400 g /14 oz canned peaches in
    natural juice
280 g/10 oz plain flour
1 tbsp baking powder
pinch of salt
115 g/4 oz caster sugar
2 eggs

175 ml/6 fl oz buttermilk
6 tbsp sunflower oil or 85 g/3 oz butter,
    melted and cooled
3 tbsp brandy
finely grated rind of 1 orange

Preheat the oven to 200°C/400°F/Gas Mark 6. Line a 12-hole muffin tin with 12 paper cases. Drain and finely chop the peaches. Sift together the flour, baking powder and salt into a large bowl. Stir in the sugar.

Place the eggs in a large jug or bowl and beat lightly, then beat in the buttermilk, oil, brandy and orange rind. Make a well in the centre of the dry ingredients, pour in the beaten liquid ingredients and add the chopped peaches. Stir gently until just combined; do not overmix. Spoon the mixture into the paper cases.

Bake in the preheated oven for 20 minutes, or until well risen, golden brown and firm to the touch. Leave to cool in the tin for 5 minutes, then serve warm or transfer to a wire rack to cool completely.

92 *Pear and liqueur muffins*

Replace the peaches with 400 g/14 oz canned pears, drained and chopped, and use Poire William liqueur to replace the brandy.

93 Warm molten-centred chocolate cupcakes

55 g/2 oz butter, softened,
or soft margarine
50 g/1¾ oz caster sugar
1 egg
85 g/3 oz self-rising flour
1 tbsp unsweetened cocoa
55 g/2 oz plain chocolate
icing sugar, for dusting

Preheat the oven to 190°C/375°F/ Gas Mark 5. Line a 12-hole muffin tin with 8 paper cases.

Place the butter, sugar, egg, flour and cocoa in a large bowl and beat together until just smooth. Spoon half of the mixture into the paper cases. Using a teaspoon, make an indentation in the centre of each cake. Break the chocolate into 8 even squares and place a piece in each indentation, then spoon the remaining cake mixture on top.

Bake in the preheated oven for 20 minutes, or until well risen and springy to the touch. Leave the cupcakes in the tin for 2–3 minutes before serving warm, dusted with sifted icing sugar.

94 White chocolate-centred cupcakes

Replace the plain chocolate with squares of white chocolate.

95 Vanilla & chocolate cupcakes

Increase the flour to 100 g/3½ oz and omit the cocoa. Add ½ teaspoon of vanilla extract to the butter and sugar, and use milk chocolate instead of the plain chocolate.

96 Chocolate cherry cupcakes

50 g/1¾ oz plain chocolate, broken
into pieces
60 g/2¼ oz butter
70 g/2½ oz cherry jam
70 g/2½ oz caster sugar
2 eggs
100 g/3½ oz self-raising flour

TOPPING
4 tsp kirsch liqueur
150 ml/5 fl oz double cream
12 fresh, glacé or
maraschino cherries
chocolate curls, to decorate

Bake in the preheated oven for 20 minutes, or until firm to the touch. Leave to cool in the tin for 10 minutes, then transfer to a wire rack to cool completely.

When the cupcakes are cold, sprinkle the kirsch over the tops of each and leave to soak for at least 15 minutes.

When ready to decorate, place the cream in a bowl and whip until soft peaks form. Spread the cream on top of the cupcakes with a knife to form the cream into peaks. Top each cupcake with a cherry and decorate with chocolate curls.

97 Chocolate strawberry cupcakes

Replace the cherry jam with strawberry jam and sprinkle the cold cupcakes with brandy instead of kirsch. Decorate each cupcake with a small whole strawberry.

Preheat the oven to 180°C/350°F/Gas Mark 4. Line a 12-hole muffin tin with 12 paper cases. Place the chocolate and butter in a saucepan and heat gently, stirring constantly, until melted. Pour into a large bowl, then stir until smooth and leave to cool slightly. Add the jam, sugar and eggs to the cooled chocolate and beat together. Add the flour and stir together until combined. Spoon the mixture into the paper cases.

Warm strawberry cupcakes baked in a tea cup

*115 g/4 oz butter, softened, plus extra
for greasing
4 tbsp strawberry jam
115 g/4 oz caster sugar
2 eggs, lightly beaten
1 tsp vanilla extract
115 g/4 oz self-raising flour
8 whole strawberries, to decorate
icing sugar, for dusting*

Preheat the oven to 180°C/350°F/Gas Mark 4. Grease six 175-ml/6-fl oz capacity heavy round tea cups with butter. Spoon 2 teaspoons of the strawberry jam into the base of each tea cup.

Place the butter and sugar in a large bowl and beat together until light and fluffy. Gradually add the eggs, beating well after each addition, then add the vanilla extract. Sift in the flour and fold into the mixture. Spoon the mixture into the tea cups.

Stand the cups in a roasting tin, then pour in enough hot water to come one third up the sides of the cups. Bake in the preheated oven for 40 minutes, or until well risen and golden brown, and a skewer, inserted in the centre, comes out clean. If overbrowning, cover the cupcakes with a sheet of foil. Leave the cupcakes to cool for 2–3 minutes, then carefully lift the cups from the tin and place them on saucers.

Top each cupcake with a strawberry, then dust them with sifted icing sugar. Serve warm with the remaining strawberries on the side.

99 *Warm raspberry cupcakes*

Replace the strawberry jam with raspberry jam and decorate with fresh raspberries.

100 *Warm peach cupcakes*

Replace the strawberry jam with a few well-drained, canned peach slices and decorate with extra peach slices.

101 *Tropical pineapple cupcakes*

*2 slices canned pineapple
in natural juice
85 g/3 oz butter, softened,
or soft margarine
100 g/3½ oz caster sugar
1 egg, lightly beaten
85 g/3 oz self-raising flour*

*FROSTING
25 g/1 oz butter, softened
115 g/4 oz soft cream cheese
grated rind of 1 lemon or lime
100 g/3½ oz icing sugar
1 tsp lemon juice or lime juice*

Preheat the oven to 180°C/350°F/ Gas Mark 4. Line a 12-hole muffin tin with 12 paper cases. Drain the pineapple, reserving the juice. Finely chop the pineapple slices. Place the butter and sugar in a large bowl and beat together until light and fluffy, then gradually beat in the egg. Add the flour and fold into the mixture. Fold in the chopped pineapple and 1 tablespoon of the reserved pineapple juice. Spoon the mixture into the paper cases. Bake in the preheated oven for 20 minutes, or until well risen and golden brown. Transfer to a wire rack to cool completely.

To make the frosting, place the butter and cream cheese in a large bowl and beat together until smooth, then add the lemon or lime rind.

Sift the icing sugar into the mixture and beat together until well mixed. Gradually beat in the lemon or lime juice, adding enough to form a spreading consistency.

When the cupcakes are cold, spread the frosting on top of each cake, or fill a piping bag fitted with a large star nozzle and pipe the frosting on top.

102 *Pina colada cupcakes*

Add 25 g/1 oz desiccated coconut and an extra ½ tablespoon of pineapple juice to the cake mixture. For the icing, beat 2 tablespoons of desiccated coconut into the icing and replace the lemon or lime juice with rum.

70 g/2½ oz plain chocolate, broken into
  pieces, plus extra to decorate
200 g/7 oz butter
150 g/5½ oz caster sugar
2 eggs, lightly beaten
2 tbsp brandy
175 g/6 oz self-raising flour

TOPPING
200 ml/7 fl oz double cream
1 tbsp icing sugar
1 tbsp brandy
9 large ripe strawberries

Preheat the oven to 180°C/350°F/Gas Mark 6. Line a 12-hole muffin
tin with 9 paper cases. Place the chocolate in a heatproof bowl, set the
bowl over a saucepan of gently simmering water and heat until melted.
Remove from the heat and leave to cool. Place the butter and sugar in a
large bowl and beat together until light and fluffy, then gradually beat
in the eggs. Stir in the brandy, followed by the melted chocolate, then
carefully fold in the flour. Spoon the mixture into the paper cases.

Bake in the preheated oven for 20–25 minutes, or until golden and
springy to the touch. Transfer to a wire rack to cool completely.

To decorate, place the cream, sugar and brandy in a bowl and whip
together until just stiff. Spoon the cream into a piping bag fitted with a
star nozzle and pipe a generous swirl of cream on top of each cake, then
place a strawberry on top.

104 *Nice & naughty cupcakes*

*Add 150 g/5½ oz raspberries to the cake mixture and decorate with extra
raspberries instead of the strawberries.*

50 g/1¼ oz butter, softened
60 g/2¼ oz demerara sugar
1 egg, lightly beaten
150 g/5½ oz plain flour
1½ tsp baking powder
½ tsp mixed spice
1 large cooking apple, peeled, cored
  and finely chopped
1 tbsp orange juice

TOPPING
5 tbsp plain flour
½ tsp mixed spice
25 g/1 oz butter
55 g/2 oz caster sugar

Preheat the oven to 180°C/350°F/
Gas Mark 4. Line a 12-hole muffin
tin with 12 paper cases.

To make the topping, place
the flour, mixed spice, butter
and sugar in a large bowl and
rub in with your fingertips
until the mixture resembles fine
breadcrumbs. Set aside.

To make the cupcakes, place
the butter and sugar in a large
bowl and beat together until light
and fluffy, then gradually beat in
the egg. Sift in the flour, baking
powder and mixed spice and fold
into the mixture, then fold in the
chopped apple and orange juice.

Spoon the mixture into the paper
cases. Add the topping to cover
the top of each cupcake and press
down gently.

Bake in the preheated oven
for 30 minutes, or until golden
brown. Leave the cupcakes to cool
in the tin for 2–3 minutes and
serve warm, or leave to cool for
10 minutes and then transfer to a
wire rack to cool completely.

1 small courgette
85 g/3 oz plain chocolate,
  broken into pieces
2 eggs
55 g/2 oz soft light brown sugar
90 ml/3 fl oz sunflower oil

115 g/4 oz plain flour
½ tsp baking powder
¼ tsp bicarbonate of soda
1 tbsp pecan nuts, finely chopped
icing sugar, for dusting

Preheat the oven to 180°C/350°F/Gas Mark 4. Line a 12-hole muffin tin with 12 paper cases. Peel and grate the courgette, discarding any liquid. Set aside.

Place the chocolate in a heatproof bowl, set the bowl over a saucepan of gently simmering water and heat until melted. Remove from the heat and stir until smooth. Leave to cool slightly.

Place the eggs, sugar and oil in a large bowl and whisk together. Sift in the flour, baking powder and bicarbonate of soda and stir together until mixed. Stir in the courgette, pecan nuts and melted chocolate until combined. Spoon the mixture into the paper cases.

Bake in the preheated oven for 25 minutes, or until firm to the touch. Leave the cupcakes to cool in the tin for 10 minutes, then transfer to a wire rack to cool completely. When the cupcakes are cold, dust with sifted icing sugar.

107 *Marbled chocolate cupcakes*   MAKES 21

175 g/6 oz soft margarine
200 g/7 oz caster sugar
3 eggs
175 g/6 oz self-raising flour
2 tbsp milk
55 g/2 oz plain chocolate, melted

Preheat the oven to 180°C/350°F/Gas Mark 4. Line two 12-hole muffin tins with 21 paper cases. Place the margarine, sugar, eggs, flour and milk in a large bowl and beat together until just smooth. Divide the mixture among 2 bowls. Add the melted chocolate to one and stir until mixed. Using a teaspoon, and alternating the chocolate mixture with the plain, put 4 half-teaspoons into each case.

Bake in the preheated oven for 20 minutes, or until well risen. Transfer to a wire rack to cool.

108 *Chocolate orange marbled cupcakes*

Add the grated rind and juice of ½ small orange and a few drops of orange food colouring to the plain cake mixture.

109 *Iced marbled cupcakes*

Make the cakes as usual. Sift 250 g/9 oz icing sugar into a bowl and stir in 2–3 tablespoons of water until smooth. Divide the icing in half and add 1 tablespoon of cocoa to one portion, adding a little extra water if required. Spoon small amounts of each icing on top of the cakes and marble together to cover the cakes with the tip of a knife.

110 *Maple pecan muffins*

280 g/10 oz plain flour
1 tbsp baking powder
pinch of salt
115 g/4 oz caster sugar
100 g/3½ oz pecan nuts, coarsely
    chopped
2 eggs

175 ml/6 fl oz buttermilk
75 ml/2½ fl oz maple syrup, plus extra
    for glazing
6 tbsp sunflower oil or 85 g/3 oz butter,
    melted and cooled
12 pecan halves

Preheat the oven to 200°C/400°F/Gas Mark 6. Line a 12-hole muffin tin with 12 paper cases. Sift together the flour, baking powder and salt into a large bowl. Stir in the sugar and pecan nuts.

Place the eggs in a large jug or bowl and beat lightly, then beat in the buttermilk, maple syrup and oil. Make a well in the centre of the dry ingredients and pour in the beaten liquid ingredients. Stir gently until just combined; do not overmix. Spoon the mixture into the paper cases and top each muffin with a pecan half.

Bake in the preheated oven for 20 minutes, or until well risen, golden brown and firm to the touch. Leave to cool in the tin for 5 minutes, then brush the tops with the maple syrup to glaze. Serve warm or transfer to a wire rack to cool completely.

111 *With maple crunch topping*

Omit the pecans from the top. Chop 150 g/5½ oz pecan nuts and mix with 3 tablespoons of brown sugar and 2 tablespoons of maple syrup, then spoon over the muffins before baking.

112 *Lemon polenta muffins*

6 tbsp sunflower oil, plus extra
    for greasing
4 lemons
about 3 tbsp low-fat natural yogurt
175 g/6 oz plain flour
1 tbsp baking powder

½ tsp bicarbonate of soda
280 g/10 oz medium polenta
115 g/4 oz caster sugar
2 eggs

Preheat the oven to 200°C/400°F/Gas Mark 6. Grease a 12-hole muffin tin. Finely grate the rind from the lemons and squeeze the juice. Add enough yogurt to make the juice up to 250 ml/9 fl oz, then stir in the lemon rind.

Sift the flour, baking powder and bicarbonate of soda into a large bowl. Stir in the polenta and sugar. Place the eggs in a large jug or bowl and beat lightly, then beat in the oil. Make a well in the centre of the dry ingredients and pour in the beaten liquid ingredients with the lemon and yogurt mixture. Stir gently until just combined; do not overmix. Spoon the mixture into the muffin tin.

Bake in the preheated oven for 20 minutes, or until well risen, golden brown and firm to the touch. Leave to cool in the tin for 5 minutes, then serve warm or transfer to a wire rack to cool completely.

113 *With Limoncello icing*

Beat 150 g/5½ oz mascarpone cheese, 50 g/1¾ oz icing sugar, and 1 tablespoon of Limoncello liqueur together and spread over the cooled muffins. Scatter over chopped candied lemon peel.

2 oranges
about 100 ml/3½ fl oz milk
280 g/10 oz plain flour
1 tbsp baking powder
pinch of salt
115 g/4 oz caster sugar

6 cardamom pods, seeds removed
    and crushed
2 eggs
6 tbsp sunflower oil or 85 g/3 oz butter,
    melted and cooled

Preheat the oven to 200°C/400°F/Gas Mark 6. Line two 24-hole mini muffin tins with 48 mini paper cases. Finely grate the rind from the oranges and squeeze the juice. Add enough milk to make the juice up to 250 ml/9 fl oz then stir in the orange rind.

Sift together the flour, baking powder and salt into a large bowl. Stir in the sugar and crushed cardamom seeds. Place the eggs in a jug and beat lightly, then beat in the orange and milk mixture and the oil. Make a well in the centre of the dry ingredients and pour in the beaten liquid ingredients. Stir gently until just combined; do not overmix. Spoon the mixture into the paper cases. Bake in the preheated oven for 15 minutes, or until well risen, golden brown and firm to the touch. Leave to cool in the tins for 5 minutes, then serve warm or transfer to a wire rack to cool completely.

115 *With white chocolate icing*

Place 150 g/5½ oz white chocolate in a heatproof bowl, set the bowl over a saucepan of simmering water and heat until melted. Stir in ½ teaspoon of orange flower water and drizzle over the muffins.

116 *Mint chocolate chip muffins*   MAKES 12

280 g/10 oz plain flour
1 tbsp baking powder
pinch of salt
115 g/4 oz caster sugar
150 g/5½ oz plain chocolate chips
2 eggs
250 ml/9 fl oz milk
6 tbsp sunflower oil or 85 g/3 oz
    butter, melted and cooled
1 tsp peppermint essence
1–2 drops of green food colouring
    (optional)
icing sugar, for dusting

Preheat the oven to 200°C/400°F/Gas Mark 6. Line a 12-hole muffin tin with 12 paper cases.

Sift together the flour, baking powder and salt into a large bowl, then stir in the caster sugar and chocolate chips. Place the eggs in a large jug or bowl and beat lightly, then beat in the milk, oil and peppermint essence. Add 1–2 drops of food colouring, if using.

Make a well in the centre of the dry ingredients and pour in the beaten liquid ingredients. Stir gently until just combined; do not overmix. Spoon the mixture into the paper cases.

Bake in the preheated oven for 20 minutes, or until well risen and firm to the touch. Leave to cool in the tin for 5 minutes, then serve warm or transfer to a wire rack to cool completely. Dust with a little sifted icing sugar before serving.

117 *With chocolate ganache*

Heat 175 ml/6 fl oz double cream in a saucepan until simmering, then pour over 175 g/6 oz chopped plain chocolate and stir until smooth. Cool and chill until thick, then spread over the muffins.

6 tbsp sunflower oil or 85 g/3 oz butter,
melted and cooled, plus extra
for greasing
280 g/10 oz plain flour
1 tbsp baking powder
4 tsp ground ginger
1½ tsp ground cinnamon

pinch of salt
115 g/4 oz soft light brown sugar
3 pieces stem ginger in syrup,
finely chopped
2 eggs
175 ml/6 fl oz milk
4 tbsp golden syrup

Preheat the oven to 200°C/400°F/Gas Mark 6. Grease a 12-hole muffin tin. Sift together the flour, baking powder, ginger, cinnamon and salt into a large bowl. Stir in the sugar and stem ginger.

Place the eggs in a large jug or bowl and beat lightly, then beat in the milk, oil and golden syrup. Make a well in the centre of the dry ingredients and pour in the beaten liquid ingredients. Stir gently until just combined; do not overmix. Spoon the mixture into the muffin tin.

Bake in the preheated oven for 20 minutes, or until well risen, golden brown and firm to the touch. Leave to cool in the tin for 5 minutes, then serve warm or transfer to a wire rack to cool completely.

119 *With lemon icing*

Sift 150 g/5½ oz icing sugar into a bowl, add 1 tablespoon of lemon juice and mix until smooth, then spread over the muffins and leave to set.

2 oranges
about 10 ml/3½ fl oz milk
225 g/8 oz plain flour
1 tbsp baking powder
pinch of salt
115 g/4 oz caster sugar
55 g/2 oz ground almonds

2 eggs
6 tbsp sunflower oil or 85 g/3 oz butter,
melted and cooled
½ tsp almond essence
40 g/1½ oz demerara sugar

Preheat the oven to 200°C/400°F/Gas Mark 6. Line a 12-hole muffin tin with 12 paper cases. Finely grate the rind from the oranges and squeeze the juice. Add enough milk to make the juice up to 250 ml/9 fl oz then stir in the orange rind. Sift together the flour, baking powder and salt into a large bowl. Stir in the caster sugar and ground almonds.

Place the eggs in a bowl and beat lightly, then beat in the orange mixture, oil and almond essence. Make a well in the centre of the dry ingredients, pour in the liquid ingredients, and mix. Spoon the mixture into the paper cases. Sprinkle the demerara sugar over the tops.

Bake in the preheated oven for 20 minutes, or until well risen, golden brown and firm to the touch. Leave to cool in the tin for 5 minutes, then serve warm or transfer to a wire rack to cool completely.

121 *With flaked almond topping*

Scatter 100 g/3½ oz flaked almonds over the muffins before they are baked.

Orange, walnut & rosemary muffins

280 g/10 oz plain flour
1 tbsp baking powder
½ tsp bicarbonate of soda
pinch of salt
115 g/4 oz caster sugar
70 g/2½ oz walnuts, coarsely chopped
2 eggs
250 ml/9 fl oz natural yogurt
6 tbsp sunflower oil or 85 g/3 oz
butter, melted and cooled
finely grated rind of 2 oranges
1 tbsp finely chopped fresh rosemary
leaves, plus extra sprigs
to decorate

ICING
175 g/6 oz icing ugar
3–4 tsp fresh orange juice
finely grated rind of ½ orange

Preheat the oven to 200°C/400°F/ Gas Mark 6. Line a 12-hole muffin tin with 12 paper cases. Sift together the flour, baking powder, bicarbonate of soda and salt into a large bowl. Stir in the caster sugar and walnuts.

Place the eggs in a large jug or bowl then beat in the yogurt, oil, orange rind and chopped rosemary leaves. Make a well in the centre of the dry ingredients and pour in the beaten liquid ingredients. Stir gently until just combined; do not overmix. Spoon the mixture into the paper cases.

Bake in the preheated oven for 20 minutes, or until well risen, golden brown and firm to the touch. Leave to cool in the tin for 5 minutes, then transfer to a wire rack to cool completely.

When the muffins are cold, make the icing. Sift the icing sugar into a bowl. Add the orange juice and orange rind and stir until the mixture is smooth and thick enough to coat the back of a wooden spoon.

Spoon the icing on top of each muffin. Decorate with a rosemary sprig and leave to set for about 30 minutes before serving.

Marbled chocolate muffins

6 tbsp sunflower oil or 85 g/3 oz butter,
melted and cooled, plus extra
for greasing
280 g/10 oz plain flour
1 tbsp baking powder
pinch of salt

115 g/4 oz caster sugar
2 eggs
250 ml/9 fl oz milk
1 tsp vanilla extract
2 tbsp cocoa powder

Preheat the oven to 200°C/400°F/Gas Mark 6. Grease a 12-hole muffin tin. Sift together the flour, baking powder and salt into a large bowl. Stir in the sugar.

Place the eggs in a large jug or bowl and beat lightly, then beat in the milk, oil and vanilla extract. Make a well in the centre of the dry ingredients and pour in the beaten liquid ingredients. Stir gently until just combined; do not overmix.

Divide the mixture between 2 bowls. Sift the cocoa into one bowl and mix together. Using teaspoons, spoon the mixtures into the muffin tin, alternating the chocolate mixture and the plain mixture.

Bake in the preheated oven for 20 minutes, or until well risen, golden brown and firm to the touch. Leave to cool in the tin for 5 minutes, then serve warm or transfer to a wire rack to cool completely.

Marbled coffee muffins

Replace the cocoa with espresso coffee powder.

150 g/5½ oz butter, softened,
  or soft margarine
150 g/5½ oz caster sugar
1 tsp vanilla extract
2 eggs, lightly beaten
140 g/5 oz self-raising flour
40 g/1½ oz cornflour

TO DECORATE
115 g/4 oz ready-to-roll fondant icing
yellow and green food colourings
300 g/10½ oz icing sugar
about 3 tbsp cold water
hundreds and thousands

Preheat the oven to 190°C/375°F/Gas Mark 5. Line two 12-hole muffin tins with 24 paper cases. Place the butter and sugar in a large bowl and beat together until light and fluffy, then beat in the vanilla extract. Gradually beat in the eggs. Sift in the flour and cornflour and fold into the mixture. Spoon the mixture into the paper cases.

Bake in the preheated oven for 12–15 minutes, or until golden and springy to the touch. Transfer to a wire rack to cool completely.

To decorate, divide the fondant icing in half and colour one half pale yellow. Roll out both halves, then use the sides of a round biscuit cutter to cut out white and yellow petal shapes. Set aside.

Sift the icing sugar into a bowl and mix with the water until smooth. Place half of the icing in a small piping bag fitted with a small plain nozzle. Divide the remaining icing in half and colour one portion yellow and the other green.

Cover 12 cakes with yellow icing and 12 with green icing. Arrange white petals on top of the yellow icing to form flowers. Pipe a little blob of white icing into the centre of each flower, then add a few hundreds and thousands on top of the white icing to form the centre of the flower. Arrange the yellow petals on the green icing and decorate in the same way. Leave to set.

175 g/6 oz self-raising flour
1 tsp baking powder
200 g/7 oz caster sugar
175 g/6 oz very soft butter,
  cut into small pieces
3 eggs
1 tsp vanilla extract
2 tbsp milk

TO DECORATE
200 g/7 oz icing sugar
1 tbsp lemon juice
1–2 tbsp water
few drops of blue and green food
  colouring
white chocolate discs
white chocolate rainbow discs
jelly bug sweets

Preheat the oven to 180°C/350°F/Gas Mark 4. Line a 12-hole muffin tin with 12 paper cases. Sift the flour, baking powder and sugar into a bowl. Add the butter, eggs, vanilla extract and milk and beat together until creamy. Spoon the mixture into the paper cases. Bake in the preheated oven for 15–20 minutes, or until risen and golden. Transfer to a wire rack to cool.

Place the icing sugar, lemon juice and water in a bowl and mix together until smooth. Colour half of the icing blue and half of the icing green. Spread the icing over the cakes. For flower cakes, place a white chocolate disc in the centre and the rainbow ones around it. For bug cakes, pipe a leaf with green icing on each cake and top with a jelly worm or bug.

175 g/6 oz butter, softened, or soft
  margarine
200 g/7 oz caster sugar
1 tsp vanilla extract
3 eggs, lightly beaten
55 g/2 oz desiccated coconut
150 g/5½ oz self-raising flour

TO DECORATE
1½ tsp cocoa powder
70 g/2½ oz icing sugar
about 300 g/10½ oz ready-to-roll
  fondant icing
food colouring, such as pink, yellow,
  brown and black

Preheat the oven to 180°C/350°F/ Gas Mark 4. Line a 12-hole muffin tin with 9 paper cases. Place the butter and sugar in a large bowl and beat together until light and fluffy, then beat in the vanilla extract. Gradually beat in the eggs, then fold in the coconut and flour. Spoon the mixture into the paper cases. Bake in the preheated oven for 20–25 minutes, or until golden and springy to the touch. Transfer to a wire rack to cool completely.

To decorate, sift the cocoa and icing sugar into a small bowl and add enough cold water to form a smooth, thick icing. Spoon into a small piping bag fitted with a writing nozzle. Leave a small piece of fondant icing white and colour a small piece pink. Divide the remainder into 2 large pieces and one smaller piece. Colour one large piece grey, using a small amount of black food colouring, and the other yellow, and the small piece brown.

To make the elephants, roll out the grey fondant and cut out 3 circles to fit the tops of the cake. To make the ears, cut out 6 circles and cut away one third of each circle. Roll out the pink fondant and cut out 6 smaller circles, then cut away one third of each circle. Place on top of the grey circles, pinch in the centre and sides and fix to the cakes with a little water. Roll a little grey fondant into a sausage shape to make the trunks and secure on the cakes with a little water. With a little white fondant, make the eyes and tusks and secure to the cake. Pipe the eyes and eyebrows with the cocoa icing.

To make the monkeys, roll and cut out 3 circles of brown fondant to fit the tops of the cake. Cut out the ears from brown fondant and make the centres of the ears with pink fondant. Secure to the cake by dampening with water. Cut out a circle of yellow fondant and cut out a small nick at the top, shape into the monkey's face and secure to the cake. Make the eyes with a little white fondant and pipe on the remaining features.

To make the lions, cut out 3 circles of yellow fondant to fit the tops of the cake. Make the ears with brown and pink fondant and secure to the cakes. Make the nose with brown fondant and pipe on the features and the curly mane.

55 g/2 oz sultanas
grated rind and juice of ½ orange
115 g/4 oz butter, softened,
  or soft margarine
115 g/4 oz caster sugar
½ tsp vanilla extract
2 eggs, lightly beaten
175 g/6 oz self-raising flour
¼ quantity buttercream
  (page 8)

TO DECORATE
250 g/9 oz icing sugar, sifted
2–3 tbsp orange juice
sugar animal cake decorations

Preheat the oven to 180°C/350°F/Gas Mark 4. Line two 12-hole muffin tins with 15 paper cases. Place the sultanas in a saucepan with the orange rind and juice and gently heat until almost boiling. Remove from the heat and leave to cool.

Place the butter and sugar in a large bowl and beat together until light and fluffy, then beat in the vanilla extract. Gradually beat in the eggs, then fold in the sultanas and the juice. Sift in the flour and fold into the mixture. Spoon the mixture into the paper cases.

Bake in the preheated oven for 15–20 minutes, or until golden and springy to the touch. Transfer to a wire rack to cool completely.

To make the icing, sift the icing sugar in a bowl and add enough orange juice to mix to a smooth coating consistency. Cover the cakes with the icing and leave to set.

To decorate, pipe a rosette of buttercream on the cakes and top with a sugar animal decoration.

175 g/6 oz butter, softened, or soft
   margarine
200 g/7 oz caster sugar
1 tsp vanilla extract
3 eggs, lightly beaten
150 g/5½ oz raspberries
225 g/8 oz self-raising flour

TO DECORATE
1 quantity buttercream (page 8)
pink, black, red and yellow food
   colouring
55–85 g/2–3 oz ready-to-roll fondant
   icing
silver dragées
jelly sweets

Preheat the oven to 180°C/350°F/Gas Mark 4. Line a 12-hole muffin tin with 10 paper cases. Place the butter and sugar in a large bowl and beat together until light and fluffy, then beat in the vanilla extract.

Gradually beat in the eggs, then fold the raspberries and flour into the mixture. Spoon the mixture into the paper cases.

Bake in the preheated oven for 20–25 minutes, or until golden brown and springy to the touch. Transfer to a wire rack to cool completely.

To decorate, colour the buttercream pale pink, then place in a piping bag fitted with a large star nozzle and pipe the buttercream on top of the cakes.

Colour the fondant icing and then mould into different shapes, such as handbags, high-heeled shoes or rings. Arrange the shapes on the cupcakes, then press silver dragées into the icing to form the handle of the bag and to decorate the shoes. Use jelly sweets to make the gems on the rings.

130 *Easy bling cupcakes*

To save time, you can decorate the cakes with non-edible cake decorations: Look out for shoes, champagne bottles or plastic rings and jewellery. Remember to remind people to remove them before eating. These would not be suitable to serve to young children.

---

131 *Gooey chocolate & cream cheese cupcakes*   MAKES 12

175 g/6 oz plain flour
20 g/¼ oz cocoa powder
¾ tsp bicarbonate of soda
200 g/7 oz caster sugar
60 ml/2 fl oz sunflower oil
175 ml/6 fl oz water

2 tsp white vinegar
½ tsp vanilla extract
150 g/5½ oz soft cream cheese
1 egg, lightly beaten
100 g/3½ oz plain chocolate chips

Preheat the oven to 180°C/350°F/Gas Mark 4. Line a 12-hole muffin tin with 12 paper cases. Sift together the flour, cocoa and bicarbonate of soda into a large bowl. Stir 150 g/5½ oz of the sugar into the flour. Add the oil, water, vinegar and vanilla extract and stir well together until combined.

Place the remaining sugar, cream cheese and egg in a large bowl and beat together until well mixed. Stir in the chocolate chips.

Spoon the chocolate mixture into the paper cases and top each with a spoonful of the cream cheese mixture.

Bake in the preheated oven for 25 minutes, or until firm to the touch. Leave the cupcakes to cool in the tin for 10 minutes, then transfer to a wire rack to cool completely.

132 Lemon cheesecake cupcakes

60 g/2¼ oz butter
125 g/4½ oz digestive biscuits, crushed
100 g/3½ oz caster sugar
280 g/10 oz soft cream cheese
2 eggs

finely grated rind of 1 large lemon
2 tsp lemon juice
125 ml/4 fl oz soured cream
4 tbsp plain flour
2 small lemons, sliced, to decorate

Preheat the oven to 160°C/325°F/Gas Mark 3. Line a 12-hole muffin tin with 12 paper cases. Place the butter in a saucepan and heat gently until melted. Remove from the heat, then add the crushed digestive biscuits and 1 tablespoon of the sugar and mix well. Divide the biscuit mixture between the paper cases and press down firmly with the back of a teaspoon. Chill in the refrigerator.

Meanwhile, place the remaining sugar, cream cheese and eggs in a large bowl and beat together until smooth. Add the lemon rind and juice, and the soured cream and beat together until combined. Add the flour and beat well. Spoon the mixture into the paper cases.

Bake in the preheated oven for 30 minutes, or until set but not browned. Leave the cupcakes to cool for 20 minutes, then transfer to a wire rack to cool completely.

When the cupcakes are cold, chill in the refrigerator for at least 3 hours. Decorate each cupcake with a twisted lemon slice.

133 Orange cheesecake cupcakes

Replace the lemon rind and juice with orange rind and juice, and decorate each cupcake with a twisted orange slice.

134 Easter cupcakes

115 g/4 oz butter, softened, or soft margarine
115 g/4 oz caster sugar
2 eggs, lightly beaten
85 g/3 oz self-raising flour
35 g/1 oz cocoa powder

TOPPING
85 g/3 oz butter, softened
115 g/4 oz icing sugar
1 tbsp milk
2–3 drops vanilla extract
260 g/9 oz mini sugar-coated chocolate eggs

Preheat the oven to 180°C/350°F/ Gas Mark 4. Line a 12-hole muffin tin with 12 paper cases.

Place the butter and sugar in a large bowl and beat together until light and fluffy, then gradually beat in the eggs. Sift in the flour and cocoa and fold into the mixture. Spoon the mixture into the paper cases.

Bake in the preheated oven for 15–20 minutes, or until well risen and firm to the touch. Transfer to a wire rack to cool.

To make the buttercream topping, place the butter in a bowl and beat until fluffy. Sift in the icing sugar and beat together until well mixed, adding the milk and vanilla extract.

When the cupcakes are cold, place the buttercream in a piping bag, fitted with a large star nozzle and pipe a circle around the edge of each cupcake to form a nest.

Place chocolate eggs in the centre of each nest to decorate.

135 Chocolate curl Easter cupcakes

Lightly sprinkle chocolate curls over the top and gently press into the buttercream topping around the edge of the cakes.

136 Really chocolatey Easter cupcakes

Add 85 g/3 oz chocolate chips to the cake mixture. Top the cupcakes with chocolate buttercream (page 8) and press chocolate shavings into the buttercream.

125 g/4½ oz butter, softened
200 g/7 oz caster sugar
4–6 drops almond essence
4 eggs, lightly beaten
150 g/5½ oz self-raising flour
175 g/6 oz ground almonds

TOPPING
450 g/1 lb white ready-to-roll fondant
　icing
55 g/2 oz green ready-to-roll coloured
　fondant icing
25 g/1 oz red ready-to-roll coloured
　fondant icing
icing sugar, for dusting

Preheat the oven to 180°C/350°F/Gas Mark 4. Line a 12-hole muffin tin with 12 paper cases. Place the butter, sugar and almond extract in a large bowl and beat together until light and fluffy, then gradually beat in the eggs. Sift in the flour and fold into the mixture, then fold in the ground almonds. Spoon the mixture into the paper cases.

Bake in the preheated oven for 20 minutes, or until well risen, golden brown and firm to the touch. Transfer to a wire rack to cool completely.

When the cupcakes are cold, knead the white fondant icing until pliable, then roll out on a surface lightly dusted with icing sugar. Cut out 12 circles with a 7-cm/2¾-inch plain round cutter, re-rolling the fondant icing as necessary. Place a circle on top of each cupcake.

Roll out the green fondant on a surface lightly dusted with icing sugar. Using the palm of your hand, rub icing sugar into the fondant to prevent it from spotting. Cut out 24 leaves with a holly leaf-shaped cutter, re-rolling the fondant icing as necessary. Brush each leaf with a little cooled boiled water and place 2 leaves on top of each cupcake. Roll the red fondant between the palms of your hands to form 36 berries and place 3 in the centre of the leaves on each cake to decorate.

138 *Spicy Christmas cupcakes*

Add 1 teaspoon of mixed spice to the cake mixture. To decorate, cover the cakes with the white ready-to-roll fondant. Use green fondant to cut out Christmas tree shapes and use yellow fondant to make a star for the top of the trees.

139 *Marzipan & fruit cupcakes*

Add 55 g/2 oz mixed dried fruit to the cake mixture. To decorate, roll out some marzipan and cut out star shapes. Brush the tops of the cakes with a little warmed apricot jam and arrange marzipan stars on top.

140 Halloween cupcakes

115 g/4 oz butter, softened,
or soft margarine
115 g/4 oz caster sugar
2 eggs
115 g/4 oz self-raising flour

TOPPING
200 g/7 oz orange ready-to-roll
coloured fondant icing
icing sugar, for dusting
55 g/2 oz black ready-to-roll
coloured fondant icing
tube of black writing icing
tube of white writing icing

Preheat the oven to 180°C/350°F/ Gas Mark 4. Line a 12-hole muffin tin with 12 paper cases. Place the butter, sugar, eggs and flour in a large bowl and beat together until smooth. Spoon the mixture into the paper cases.

Bake in the preheated oven for 15–20 minutes, or until well risen, golden and firm to the touch. Transfer to a wire rack to cool.

When the cupcakes are cold, knead the orange fondant icing until pliable, then roll out on a surface dusted with icing sugar. Rub icing sugar into the fondant icing to prevent it from spotting. Cut out 12 circles with a 5.5-cm/ 2¼-inch round cutter, re-rolling the fondant icing as necessary. Place a circle on top of each cake. Roll out the black fondant icing on a surface dusted with icing sugar. Rub icing sugar into the fondant icing to prevent it from spotting. Cut out 12 circles with a 3-cm/1¼-inch round cutter and place them in the centre of the cakes. Using black writing icing, pipe 8 legs onto each spider and draw eyes and a mouth with white icing.

141 Pumpkin-decorated cupcakes

Cover the cakes with white fondant icing. Use orange fondant icing to cut out and make pumpkin shapes. Pipe on the stems of the pumpkins with green writing icing and pipe a jagged mouth and eyes on the pumpkin with black writing icing.

142 Spider web cupcakes

Melt 55 g/2 oz plain chocolate and spoon into a piping bag fitted with a writing nozzle. Cover the cakes with glacé icing (page 8). Pipe rounds of chocolate onto the cakes and, using a skewer, quickly drag the chocolate from the centre to the outside of the cakes several times to feather the icing and chocolate into a spider web design.

143 Valentine heart cupcakes

85 g/3 oz butter, softened,
or soft margarine
100 g/3½ oz caster sugar
½ tsp vanilla extract
2 eggs, lightly beaten
70 g/2½ oz plain flour
1 tbsp cocoa powder
1 tsp baking powder

MARZIPAN HEARTS
icing sugar, for dusting
35 g/1¼ oz marzipan
red food colouring (liquid or paste)

TOPPING
55 g/2 oz butter, softened
115 g/4 oz icing sugar
25 g/1 oz plain chocolate, melted
6 chocolate flower decorations

To make the hearts, line a baking sheet with baking paper and lightly dust with icing sugar. Knead the marzipan until pliable, then add a few drops of red colouring and knead until evenly coloured. Roll out the marzipan to a thickness of 5 mm/¼ inch on a surface dusted with icing sugar. Cut out 6 hearts with a small heart-shaped cutter and place on the sheet. Leave for 3–4 hours.

To make the cupcakes, preheat the oven to 180°C/350°F/Gas Mark 4. Line a 12-hole muffin tin with 6 paper cases. Place the butter, sugar and vanilla extract in a large bowl and beat together until light and fluffy, then gradually beat in the eggs. Sift in the flour, cocoa and baking powder and fold into the mixture. Spoon the mixture into the paper cases. Bake in the preheated oven for 20–25 minutes, or until well risen and firm to the touch. Transfer to a wire rack to cool completely.

To make the topping, place the butter in a bowl and beat until fluffy. Sift in the icing sugar and beat until smooth. Add the melted chocolate and beat until mixed. Spread the icing on top of each cake and decorate with a chocolate flower and a heart.

144 Cherry & vanilla heart cupcakes

Increase the vanilla extract to 1 teaspoon and the flour to 90 g/3¼ oz. Omit the cocoa and add 40 g/1½ oz quartered glacé cherries. Decorate with vanilla buttercream instead of chocolate buttercream.

145 Gold & silver anniversary cupcakes

225 g/8 oz butter, softened
225 g/8 oz caster sugar
1 tsp vanilla extract
4 eggs, lightly beaten
225 g/8 oz self-raising flour
5 tbsp milk

TOPPING
175 g/6 oz butter
350 g/12 oz icing sugar
silver or gold dragées

Preheat the oven to 180°C/350°F/Gas Mark 4. Line two 12-hole muffin tins with 24 silver or gold foil cake cases. Place the butter, sugar and vanilla extract in a large bowl and beat together until light and fluffy, then gradually beat in the eggs. Sift in the flour and fold into the mixture with the milk. Spoon the mixture into the foil cases.

Bake in the preheated oven for 15–20 minutes, or until well risen and firm to the touch. Transfer to a wire rack to cool completely.

To make the topping, place the butter in a large bowl and beat until fluffy. Sift in the icing sugar and beat together until well mixed. Place the topping in a piping bag fitted with a medium star-shaped nozzle.

When the cupcakes are cold, pipe circles of icing on top of each cake to cover the tops and sprinkle over the silver or gold dragées.

146 Ruby wedding cupcakes

Add 55 g/2 oz quartered glacé cherries to the cake mixture and decorate as before using red dragées.

147 Rocky mountain cupcakes

200 g/7 oz butter, softened,
    or soft margarine
140 g/5 oz caster sugar
1 tsp vanilla extract
3 eggs, lightly beaten
150 g/5½ oz self-raising flour
55 g/2 oz cocoa powder

TOPPING
1 quantity chocolate buttercream
    (page 8)
85 g/3 oz mini marshmallows
55 g/2 oz walnuts, coarsely chopped
55 g/2 oz milk chocolate or plain
    chocolate, broken into pieces

Preheat the oven to 180°C/350°F/Gas Mark 4. Line a 12-hole muffin tin with 10 paper cases. Place the butter and sugar in a large bowl and beat together until light and fluffy, then beat in the vanilla extract. Gradually beat in the eggs. Sift the flour and cocoa together and fold into the mixture. Spoon the mixture into the paper cases.

Bake in the preheated oven for 20–25 minutes, or until golden and springy to the touch. Transfer to a wire rack to cool completely.

To decorate, pipe the buttercream on top of each cake to form a peak in the centre. Mix the marshmallows and walnuts together and divide between the cakes, then press down lightly. Place the chocolate in a heatproof bowl, set the bowl over a pan of gently simmering water and heat until melted. Drizzle over the tops of the cakes and leave to set.

400 g/14 oz butter, softened
400 g/14 oz caster sugar
finely grated rind of 2 lemons
8 eggs, lightly beaten
400 g/14 oz self-raising flour

TOPPING
350 g/12 oz icing sugar
6–8 tsp hot water
red or blue food colouring
 (liquid or paste)
24 sugared almonds

Preheat the oven to 180°C/350°F/Gas Mark 4. Line two 12-hole muffin tins with 24 paper cases. Place the butter, sugar and lemon rind in a large bowl and beat together until light and fluffy, then gradually beat in the eggs. Sift in the flour and fold into the mixture. Spoon the mixture into the paper cases.

Bake in the preheated oven for 20–25 minutes, or until well risen, golden brown and firm to the touch. Transfer to a wire rack to cool.

When the cakes are cold, make the topping. Sift the icing sugar into a bowl, add the hot water and stir until smooth and thick enough to coat the back of a wooden spoon. Dip a skewer into the red or blue food colouring and stir it into the icing until it is evenly coloured pink or pale blue. Spoon the icing on top of each cake. Top each with a sugared almond and leave to set for about 30 minutes.

149 *Scented baby shower cupcakes*

Omit the lemon rind and add 1 tablespoon of chopped lavender or rosemary to the cake mixture after beating in the eggs. Decorate as before or with confetti-type sprinkles.

150 *Chocolate brownie cupcakes*   MAKES 12

225 g/8 oz plain chocolate,
 broken into pieces
85 g/3 oz butter
2 eggs
200 g/7 oz soft dark brown sugar

1 tsp vanilla extract
140 g/5 oz plain flour
75 g/2¼ oz walnuts, chopped into
 small pieces

Preheat the oven to 180°C/350°F/Gas Mark 4. Line a 12-hole muffin tin with 12 paper cases. Place the chocolate and butter in a saucepan and heat gently, stirring constantly, until melted. Remove from the heat and stir until smooth. Leave to cool slightly.

Place the eggs and sugar in a large bowl and whisk together, then add the vanilla extract. Stir in the flour until mixed together, then stir the melted chocolate into the mixture until combined. Stir in the chopped walnuts. Spoon the mixture into the paper cases.

Bake in the preheated oven for 30 minutes, or until firm to the touch but still slightly moist in the centre. Leave the cupcakes to cool for 10 minutes, then transfer to a wire rack to cool completely.

151   *High-fibre muffins*

140 g/5 oz high-fibre bran cereal
250 ml/9 fl oz skimmed milk
140 g/5 oz plain flour
1 tbsp baking powder
1 tsp ground cinnamon
½ tsp freshly grated nutmeg

115 g/4 oz caster sugar
100 g/3½ oz raisins
2 eggs
6 tbsp sunflower oil

Preheat the oven to 200°C/400°F/Gas Mark 6. Line a 12-hole muffin tin with 12 paper cases. Put the cereal and milk in a bowl and leave to soak for about 5 minutes, or until the cereal has softened.

Meanwhile, sift together the flour, baking powder, cinnamon and nutmeg into a large bowl. Stir in the sugar and raisins.

Place the eggs in a large jug or bowl and beat lightly, then beat in the oil. Make a well in the centre of the dry ingredients and pour in the beaten liquid ingredients and the cereal mixture. Stir gently until just combined; do not overmix. Spoon the mixture into the paper cases.

Bake in the preheated oven for 20 minutes, or until well risen, golden brown and firm to the touch. Leave to cool in the tin for 5 minutes, then serve warm or transfer to a wire rack to cool completely.

152   *High-fibre seed muffins*

Add 3 tablespoons of chopped mixed seeds, such as pumpkin, sunflower and hemp seeds with the raisins.

153   *Sunflower seed muffins*

140 g/5 oz plain flour
1 tbsp baking powder
115 g/4 oz soft light brown sugar
140 g/5 oz porridge oats
100 g/3½ oz sultanas
125 g/4½ oz sunflower seeds

2 eggs
250 ml/9 fl oz skimmed milk
6 tbsp sunflower oil
1 tsp vanilla extract

Preheat the oven to 200°C/400°F/Gas Mark 6. Line a 12-hole muffin tin with 12 paper cases. Sift together the flour and baking powder into a large bowl. Stir in the sugar, oats, sultanas and 55 g/2 oz of the sunflower seeds.

Place the eggs in a large jug or bowl and beat lightly, then beat in the milk, oil and vanilla extract. Make a well in the centre of the dry ingredients and pour in the beaten liquid ingredients. Stir gently until just combined; do not overmix. Spoon the mixture into the paper cases. Sprinkle the remaining sunflower seeds over the tops of the muffins.

Bake in the preheated oven for 20 minutes, or until well risen, golden brown and firm to the touch. Leave to cool in the tin for 5 minutes, then serve warm or transfer to a wire rack to cool completely.

154 Muesli muffins

140 g/5 oz plain flour
1 tbsp baking powder
280 g/10 oz unsweetened muesli
115 g/4 oz soft light brown sugar

2 eggs
250 ml/9 fl oz buttermilk
6 tbsp sunflower oil

Preheat the oven to 200°C/400°F/Gas Mark 6. Line a 12-hole muffin tin with 12 paper cases. Sift together the flour and baking powder into a large bowl. Stir in the muesli and sugar.

Place the eggs in a large jug or bowl and beat lightly, then beat in the buttermilk and oil. Make a well in the centre of the dry ingredients and pour in the beaten liquid ingredients. Stir gently until just combined; do not overmix. Spoon the mixture into the paper cases.

Bake in the preheated oven for 20 minutes, or until well risen, golden brown and firm to the touch. Leave to cool in the tin for 5 minutes, then serve warm or transfer to a wire rack to cool completely.

155 Apple & muesli muffins

Add 50 g/1¾ oz chopped dried apple to the muffin mixture and add a dried apple ring to the top of each muffin before baking.

156 Wheatgerm, banana & pumpkin seed muffins

6 tbsp sunflower oil, plus extra
    for greasing
140 g/5 oz plain flour
1 tbsp baking powder
115 g/4 oz caster sugar
140 g/5 oz wheatgerm

85 g/3 oz pumpkin seeds
2 bananas
about 150 ml/5 fl oz skimmed milk
2 eggs

Preheat the oven to 200°C/400°F/Gas Mark 6. Grease a 12-hole muffin tin. Sift together the flour and baking powder into a large bowl. Stir in the sugar, wheatgerm and 40 g/1½ oz of the pumpkin seeds. Mash the bananas and place in a jug, then add enough milk to make up the purée to 250 ml/9 fl oz.

Place the eggs in a large jug or bowl and beat lightly, then beat in the banana and milk mixture and the oil. Make a well in the centre of the dry ingredients and pour in the beaten liquid ingredients. Stir gently until just combined; do not overmix. Spoon the mixture into the muffin tin. Sprinkle the remaining pumpkin seeds over the top.

Bake in the preheated oven for 20 minutes, or until well risen, golden brown and firm to the touch. Leave to cool in the tin for 5 minutes, then serve warm or transfer to a wire rack to cool completely.

157 With crunchy topping

Chop 2 tablespoons of pumpkin seeds and 85 g/3 oz banana chips and mix with 2 tablespoons of soft brown sugar. Scatter over the muffins before baking.

Wholemeal banana muffins

50 g/1¾ oz raisins
3 tbsp fresh orange juice
140 g/5 oz plain flour
140 g/5 oz wholemeal flour
1 tbsp baking powder
115 g/4 oz caster sugar
2 bananas

about 90ml/3 fl oz skimmed milk
2 eggs
6 tbsp sunflower oil
finely grated rind of 1 orange

Put the raisins in a bowl, add the orange juice and leave to soak for 1 hour. Preheat the oven to 200°C/400°F/Gas Mark 6. Line a 12-hole muffin tin with 12 paper cases.

Sift together both types of flour and the baking powder into a large bowl, adding any bran left in the sieve. Stir in the sugar.

Mash the bananas and place in a jug, then add enough milk to make up the purée to 200 ml/7 fl oz. Place the eggs in a large jug or bowl and beat lightly, then beat in the banana and milk mixture, oil, soaked raisins and orange rind. Make a well in the centre of the dry ingredients and pour in the beaten liquid ingredients. Stir gently until just combined; do not overmix. Spoon the mixture into the paper cases.

Bake in the preheated oven for 20 minutes, or until well risen, golden brown and firm to the touch. Leave to cool in the tin for 5 minutes, then serve warm or transfer to a wire rack to cool completely.

159 With banana topping

Mash 1 ripe banana with ½ teaspoon of lemon juice. Beat 150 g/5½ oz cream cheese with 2 tablespoons of icing sugar and mix in the banana, then spread over the muffins.

160 Yogurt & spice muffins

140 g/5 oz wholemeal flour
140 g/5 oz plain flour
1 tbsp baking powder
½ tsp bicarbonate of soda
4 tsp mixed spice
115 g/4 oz caster sugar

100 g/3½ oz mixed dried fruit
2 eggs
250 ml/9 fl oz low-fat natural yogurt
6 tbsp sunflower oil

Preheat the oven to 200°C/400°F/Gas Mark 6. Line a 12-hole muffin tin with 12 paper cases. Sift together both types of flour, the baking powder, bicarbonate of soda and mixed spice into a large bowl, adding any bran left in the sieve. Stir in the sugar and dried fruit.

Place the eggs in a large jug or bowl and beat lightly, then beat in the yogurt and oil. Make a well in the centre of the dry ingredients and pour in the beaten liquid ingredients. Stir gently until just combined; do not overmix. Spoon the mixture into the paper cases.

Bake in the preheated oven for 20 minutes, or until well risen, golden brown and firm to the touch. Leave to cool in the tin for 5 minutes, then serve warm or transfer to a wire rack to cool completely.

161 Vanilla & spice muffins

Omit the dried fruit and use vanilla yogurt and the seeds from a vanilla pod.

6 tbsp sunflower oil, plus extra
    for greasing
70 g/2½ oz wholemeal flour
70 g/2½ oz plain flour
1 tbsp baking powder
115 g/4 oz soft dark brown sugar

60 g/2¼ oz medium polenta
70 g/2½ oz porridge oats
2 eggs
250 ml/9 fl oz buttermilk
1 tsp vanilla extract

Preheat the oven to 200°C/400°F/Gas Mark 6. Grease a 12-hole muffin tin. Sift together the flours and the baking powder into a large bowl, adding any bran left in the sieve. Stir in the sugar, polenta and oats.

Place the eggs in a large jug or bowl and beat lightly, then beat in the buttermilk, oil and vanilla extract. Make a well in the centre of the dry ingredients and pour in the beaten liquid ingredients. Stir gently until just combined; do not overmix. Spoon the mixture into the muffin tin.

Bake in the preheated oven for 20 minutes, or until well risen, golden brown and firm to the touch. Leave to cool in the tin for 5 minutes, then serve warm or transfer to a wire rack to cool completely.

6 tbsp sunflower oil or 85 g/3 oz butter,
    melted and cooled, plus extra
    for greasing
175 g/6 oz plain flour
1 tbsp baking powder
pinch of salt

freshly ground black pepper
115 g/4 oz medium polenta
2 eggs
250 ml/9 fl oz milk
175 g/6 oz frozen sweetcorn kernels

Preheat the oven to 200°C/400°F/Gas Mark 6. Grease a 12-hole muffin tin. Sift together the flour, baking powder, salt and pepper to taste into a large bowl. Stir in the polenta.

Place the eggs in a large jug or bowl and beat lightly, then beat in the milk and oil. Make a well in the centre of the dry ingredients, pour in the beaten liquid ingredients and add the sweetcorn. Stir gently until just combined; do not overmix. Spoon the mixture into the muffin tin.

Bake in the preheated oven for 20 minutes, or until well risen, golden brown and firm to the touch. Leave to cool in the tin for 5 minutes, then serve warm or transfer to a wire rack to cool completely.

164 Cranberry & almond muffins

6 tbsp sunflower oil or 85 g/3 oz butter,
    melted and cooled, plus extra
    for greasing
225 g/8 oz plain flour
1 tbsp baking powder
pinch of salt
115 g/4 oz caster sugar
55 g/2 oz ground almonds

2 eggs
250 ml/9 fl oz buttermilk
½ tsp almond essence
150 g/5½ oz fresh or frozen cranberries
40 g/1½ oz demerara sugar
40 g/1½ oz flaked almonds

Preheat the oven to 200°C/400°F/Gas Mark 6. Grease a 12-hole muffin tin. Sift together the flour, baking powder and salt into a large bowl. Stir in the caster sugar and ground almonds.

Place the eggs in a large jug or bowl and beat lightly, then beat in the buttermilk, oil and almond essence. Make a well in the centre of the dry ingredients, pour in the beaten liquid ingredients and add the cranberries. Stir gently until just combined; do not overmix. Spoon the mixture into the muffin tin. Sprinkle the demerara sugar and flaked almonds over the tops of the muffins.

Bake in the preheated oven for 20 minutes, or until well risen, golden brown and firm to the touch. Leave to cool in the tin for 5 minutes, then serve warm or transfer to a wire rack to cool completely.

165 With almond crunch topping

Chop the flaked almonds and mix with the demerara sugar and 4 crushed amaretti biscuits, then sprinkle the mixture over the top of the muffins before baking.

166 Fresh flower muffins

280 g/10 oz plain flour
1 tbsp baking powder
pinch of salt
115 g/4 oz caster sugar
2 eggs
250 ml/9 fl oz buttermilk
6 tbsp sunflower oil or 85 g/3 oz butter,
    melted and cooled
finely grated rind of 1 lemon

TOPPING
85 g/3 oz butter, softened
175 g/6 oz icing sugar
12 edible flower heads, such as lavender,
    nasturtiums, violets, primroses or
    roses, to decorate

Preheat the oven to 200°C/400°F/Gas Mark 6. Line a 12-hole muffin tin with 12 paper cases. Carefully wash the flower heads and leave to dry on kitchen paper.

Sift together the flour, baking powder and salt into a large bowl. Stir in the sugar. Place the eggs in a large jug or bowl and beat lightly, then beat in the buttermilk, oil and lemon rind. Make a well in the centre of the dry ingredients and pour in the beaten liquid ingredients. Stir gently until just combined; do not overmix. Spoon the mixture into the paper cases.

Bake in the preheated oven for 20 minutes, or until well risen, golden brown and firm to the touch. Leave to cool in the tin for 5 minutes, then transfer to a wire rack to cool completely.

To make the icing, place the butter in a large bowl and beat until fluffy. Sift in the icing sugar and beat together until smooth, then place in a piping bag fitted with a large star nozzle and pipe circles on top of each muffin. Just before serving, place a flower head on top to decorate.

167 Sugar rose petal muffins

Brush 12 fresh rose petals with beaten egg white and dredge in caster sugar, place on baking paper to dry, and use to decorate the muffins.

168 *Fresh orange muffins*

6 tbsp sunflower oil, plus extra
    for greasing
5 oranges
140 g/5 oz wholemeal flour
140 g/5 oz plain flour

1 tbsp baking powder
115 g/4 oz caster sugar
2 eggs
250 ml/9 fl oz fresh orange juice

Preheat the oven to 200°C/400°F/ Gas Mark 6. Grease a 12-hole muffin tin. Grate the rind from 2 of the oranges and set aside. Remove the peel from all of the oranges, discarding the white pith. Cut the flesh into segments, reserving 6 segments. Cut the reserved segments in half and set aside. Cut the remaining segments into small pieces.

Sift together both types of flour and the baking powder into a large bowl, adding any bran left in the sieve. Stir in the sugar.

Place the eggs in a large jug or bowl and beat lightly, then beat in the orange juice, oil and reserved orange rind.

Make a well in the centre of the dry ingredients, pour in the beaten liquid ingredients and add the chopped oranges. Stir until combined; do not overmix. Spoon the mixture into the muffin tin.

Place the halved orange segments on the top.

Bake in the preheated oven for 20 minutes, or until well risen, golden brown and firm to the touch. Cool for 5 minutes, then serve warm or transfer to a wire rack to cool completely.

169 *Fresh peach muffins*

Stone and peel 5 fresh peaches and proceed as for the oranges. Replace the orange juice with peach nectar.

170 *Fresh strawberry & cream muffins*

6 tbsp sunflower oil or 85 g/3 oz butter,
    melted and cooled, plus extra
    for greasing
150 g/5½ oz strawberries
280 g/10 oz plain flour
1 tbsp baking powder
pinch of salt
115 g/4 oz caster sugar

2 eggs
250 ml/9 fl oz single cream
1 tsp vanilla extract

TOPPING
125 ml/4 fl oz double cream
12 whole small strawberries,
    to decorate

Preheat the oven to 200°C/400°F/ Gas Mark 6. Grease a 12-hole muffin tin. Chop the strawberries into small pieces. Sift together the flour, baking powder and salt into a large bowl. Stir in the sugar and chopped strawberries.

Place the eggs in a large jug or bowl and lightly beat, then beat in the single cream, oil and vanilla extract. Make a well in the centre of the dry ingredients and pour in the beaten liquid ingredients.

Stir gently until just combined; do not overmix. Spoon the mixture into the muffin tin.

Bake in the preheated oven for 20 minutes until well risen, golden brown and firm to the touch. Leave to cool in the tin for 5 minutes, then transfer to a wire rack to cool completely.

Place the double cream in a bowl and whip until stiff. When the muffins are cold, pipe or spread the cream on top of each muffin, then top with a small strawberry.

171 *With sweet wine & strawberry topping*

Hull and slice the strawberries, pour over 2 tablespoons of sweet white wine, and leave to macerate for 10 minutes before spooning a few strawberry slices onto each muffin.

24-carrot gold cupcakes

175 g/6 oz butter, softened, or soft
  margarine
115 g/4 oz caster sugar
2 eggs, lightly beaten
300 g/10 oz carrots, grated
55 g/2 oz walnuts, finely chopped
2 tbsp orange juice
grated rind of ½ orange

175 g/6 oz self-raising flour
1 tsp ground cinnamon
12 walnut halves, to decorate

FROSTING
115 g/4 oz cream cheese
225 g/8 oz icing sugar
1 tbsp orange juice

Preheat the oven to 180°C/350°F/Gas Mark 4. Line a 12-hole muffin tin with 12 paper cases. Place the butter and sugar in a large bowl and beat together until light and fluffy, then gradually beat in the eggs. Fold in the grated carrot, walnuts and orange juice and rind. Sift in the flour and cinnamon and fold into the mixture until just combined. Spoon the mixture into the paper cases.

Bake in the preheated oven for 15–20 minutes, or until golden and springy to the touch. Transfer to a wire rack to cool completely.

To make the frosting, place the cream cheese, icing sugar and orange juice in a bowl and beat together. Spread over the top of the cakes, then decorate with walnut halves.

173 ## 9-carrot gold cupcakes

Use 85 g/3 oz grated carrot and 85 g/3 oz grated courgette, and replace the walnuts with 55 g/2 oz sultanas. Decorate the top of each cake with a pecan.

Pure indulgence almond cupcakes

100 g/3½ oz butter, softened
100 g/3½ oz caster sugar
2 eggs, lightly beaten
¼ tsp almond essence
4 tbsp single cream
175 g/6 oz plain flour
1½ tsp baking powder
70 g/2½ oz ground almonds

TOPPING
115 g/4 oz butter, softened
225 g/8 oz icing sugar
few drops of almond essence
25 g/1 oz toasted flaked almonds

Preheat the oven to 180°C/350°F/Gas Mark 4. Line a 12-hole muffin tin with 12 paper cases. Place the butter and sugar in a large bowl and beat together until light and fluffy. Gradually beat in the eggs, then add the almond essence and cream. Sift in the flour and baking powder and fold into the mixture, then fold in the ground almonds. Spoon the mixture into the paper cases.

Bake in the preheated oven for 25 minutes, or until golden brown and firm to the touch. Leave the cupcakes to cool in the tin for 10 minutes, then transfer to a wire rack to cool completely.

To make the icing, place the butter in a large bowl and beat until creamy. Sift in the icing sugar. Add the almond essence and beat until smooth. Spread the icing on top of each cake, using a knife to form the icing into swirls. Sprinkle the almonds over the top.

175 Ice-cream cone cupcakes

175 g/6 oz butter, softened, or soft
    margarine
200 g/7 oz caster sugar
1 tsp vanilla extract
3 eggs, lightly beaten
55 g/2 oz ground almonds
150 g/5½ oz self-raising flour

TOPPING
1 quantity buttercream
    (page 8)
8 mini chocolate bars
sugar sprinkles
seedless raspberry jam (optional)

Preheat the oven to 180°C/350°F/Gas Mark 4. Line a 12-hole muffin tin with 8 paper cases. Place the butter and sugar in a large bowl and beat together until light and fluffy, then beat in the vanilla extract. Gradually beat in the eggs, then fold in the almonds and flour. Spoon the mixture into the paper cases, peaking the mixture slightly in the middle.

Bake in the preheated oven for 20–25 minutes, or until golden and springy to the touch. Transfer to a wire rack to cool completely.

Spoon the buttercream into a piping bag fitted with a large star nozzle and pipe the buttercream over the cakes to peak like an ice-cream cone. Press a chocolate bar into each cake and scatter a few sprinkles on top. Warm the raspberry jam and drizzle a little over each cake, if liked.

176 Chocolate ice-cream cone cupcakes

Replace 2 tablespoons of flour with cocoa. Decorate with chocolate buttercream (page 8), chocolate sprinkles and a drizzle of chocolate sauce.

177 Buttermilk & orange cupcakes

55 g/2 oz soft dark brown sugar
250 g/9 oz butter, softened
2 eggs, lightly beaten
200 g/7 oz plain flour
¼ tsp baking powder
½ tsp bicarbonate of soda

125 ml/4 fl oz buttermilk

ICING
225 g/8 oz icing sugar
finely grated rind of 2 oranges,
    plus 1 tbsp juice

Preheat the oven to 180°C/350°F/Gas Mark 4. Line a 12-hole muffin tin with 12 paper cases. Place the brown sugar and 125 g/4½ oz of the butter in a large bowl and beat together until light and fluffy, then gradually beat in the eggs. Sift in the flour, baking powder and bicarbonate of soda and fold into the mixture, then fold in the buttermilk and grated orange rind of 1 orange. Spoon the mixture into the paper cases.

Bake in the preheated oven for 30 minutes, or until firm to the touch. Leave the cupcakes to cool in the tin for 10 minutes, then transfer to a wire rack to cool completely.

To make the icing, place the remaining butter in a large bowl and beat until fluffy. Sift in the icing sugar. Add the remaining orange rind and the juice and beat together until smooth.

When the cupcakes are cold, spread the icing on top, using a knife to form the icing into swirls.

115 g/4 oz butter, softened
115 g/4 oz caster sugar
2 eggs, lightly beaten
115 g/4 oz self-raising flour
finely grated rind of 1 lemon
1 tbsp lemon curd
100 g/3½ oz fresh raspberries

TOPPING
25 g/1 oz butter
1 tbsp soft light brown sugar
1 tbsp ground almonds
1 tbsp plain flour

Preheat the oven to 200°C/400°F/Gas Mark 6. Line a 12-hole muffin tin with 12 paper cases. To make the topping, place the butter in a saucepan and heat gently until melted. Pour into a bowl and add the sugar, ground almonds and flour and stir together until combined.

To make the cupcakes, place the butter and sugar in a large bowl and beat together until light and fluffy, then gradually add the eggs. Sift in the flour and fold into the mixture. Fold in the lemon rind, lemon curd and raspberries. Spoon the mixture into the paper cases. Add the topping to cover the top of each cupcake and press down gently.

Bake in the preheated oven for 15–20 minutes, or until golden brown and firm to the touch. Leave the cupcakes to cool for 10 minutes, then transfer to a wire rack to cool completely.

300 g/10½ oz plain chocolate, broken
   into pieces
150 g/5½ oz butter, cut into cubes
175 g/6 oz golden syrup
100 g/3½ oz Brazil nuts, coarsely
   chopped

100 g/3½ oz ready-to-eat dried raisins
200 g/7 oz cornflakes
18 glacé cherries, to decorate

Place 18 paper cases on a baking sheet. Place the chocolate, butter and golden syrup into a large saucepan and heat gently until the butter has melted and the ingredients are runny but not hot. Remove from the heat and stir until well mixed.

Add the chopped nuts and raisins to the pan and stir together until the fruit and nuts are covered in chocolate. Add the cornflakes and stir until combined.

Spoon the mixture evenly into the paper cases and top each with a glacé cherry. Leave to set in a cool place for 2–4 hours before serving.

Devil's food cake with chocolate frosting

50 g/1¾ oz butter, softened,
    or soft margarine
115 g/4 oz soft dark brown sugar
2 eggs
115 g/4 oz plain flour
½ tsp bicarbonate of soda
25 g/1 oz cocoa powder
125 ml/4 fl oz soured cream

FROSTING
125 g/4½ oz plain chocolate, broken
    into pieces
2 tbsp caster sugar
150 ml/5 fl oz soured cream

CHOCOLATE STICKS (optional)
100 g/3½ oz plain chocolate

Preheat the oven to 180°C/350°F/Gas Mark 4. Line two 12-hole muffin tins with 18 paper cases. Place the butter, sugar, eggs, flour, bicarbonate of soda and cocoa in a large bowl and beat together until just smooth. Fold in the soured cream. Spoon the mixture into the paper cases.

Bake in the preheated oven for 20 minutes, or until well risen and firm to the touch. Transfer to a wire rack to cool completely.

To make the frosting, place the chocolate in a heatproof bowl, set the bowl over a saucepan of gently simmering water and heat until melted. Leave to cool slightly, then whisk in the sugar and soured cream until combined. Spread the frosting over the tops of the cakes and leave to chill in the refrigerator before serving.

Decorate with chocolate sticks made by shaving plain chocolate with a vegetable peeler, if liked.

Strawberry shortcakes

85 g/3 oz butter, plus extra
    for greasing
225 g/8 oz self-raising flour, plus
    extra for dusting
½ tsp baking powder
100 g/3½ oz caster sugar
1 egg, lightly beaten
2–3 tbsp milk, plus extra for brushing

FILLING
1 tsp vanilla extract
250 g/9 oz mascarpone cheese
3 tbsp icing sugar, plus extra for
    dusting
400 g/14 oz strawberries

Preheat the oven to 180°C/350°F/Gas Mark 4. Lightly grease a large baking sheet. Sift the flour, baking powder and sugar into a bowl. Add the butter and rub it in with your fingertips until the mixture resembles breadcrumbs.

Place the egg and 2 tablespoons of the milk in a bowl and beat together, then stir in the dry ingredients with a fork to form a soft, but not sticky, dough, adding more milk if necessary. Turn the dough out onto a lightly floured work surface and roll out to about 2 cm/¾ inch thick. Cut out rounds with a 7-cm/2¾-inch biscuit cutter. Press the trimmings together and cut out more rounds until you have 6 rounds. Place the rounds on the baking sheet and brush with milk.

Bake in the preheated oven for 12–15 minutes, until firm and golden brown. Transfer to a wire rack to cool.

To make the filling, stir the vanilla extract into the mascarpone cheese with 2 tablespoons of the icing sugar. Set aside a few whole strawberries, then slice the rest. Sprinkle with the remaining tablespoon of icing sugar. Split the shortcakes in half horizontally.

Spoon half the mascarpone mixture onto the bases and top with sliced strawberries. Spoon over the remaining mascarpone mixture and cover with the tops. Dust with icing sugar and top with the strawberries.

Raspberry shortcakes

Replace the strawberries with whole raspberries and sandwich with the mascarpone filling.

183 Chocolate muffins

225 g/8 oz plain flour
55 g/2 oz cocoa powder
1 tbsp baking powder
pinch of salt
115 g/4 oz soft light brown sugar
2 eggs

200 ml/7 fl oz soured cream
6 tbsp sunflower oil or 85 g/3 oz butter,
    melted and cooled
3 tbsp golden syrup

Preheat the oven to 200°C/400°F/Gas Mark 6. Line a 12-hole muffin tin with 12 paper cases. Sift together the flour, cocoa, baking powder and salt into a large bowl. Stir in the sugar.

Place the eggs in a large jug or bowl and beat lightly, then beat in the soured cream, oil and golden syrup. Make a well in the centre of the dry ingredients and pour in the beaten liquid ingredients. Stir gently until just combined; do not overmix. Spoon the mixture into the paper cases.

Bake in the preheated oven for 20 minutes, or until well risen and firm to the touch. Leave to cool in the tin for 5 minutes, then serve warm or transfer to a wire rack to cool completely.

184 Sticky toffee muffins

6 tbsp sunflower oil or 85 g/3 oz butter,
    melted and cooled, plus extra
    for greasing
250 g/9 oz stoned dates
250 ml/9 fl oz water
280 g/10 oz plain flour
1 tbsp baking powder

pinch of salt
115 g/4 oz soft dark brown sugar
2 eggs
4 tbsp dulce de leche (from a jar),
    to serve

Preheat the oven to 200°C/400°F/Gas Mark 6. Grease a 12-hole muffin tin. Put the dates and water in a food processor and blend to form a coarse purée. Sift together the flour, baking powder and salt into a large bowl. Stir in the sugar.

Place the eggs in a large jug or bowl and beat lightly, then beat in the date purée and oil. Make a well in the centre of the dry ingredients and pour in the beaten liquid ingredients. Stir gently until just combined; do not overmix. Spoon the mixture into the muffin tin.

Bake in the preheated oven for 20 minutes, or until golden brown and firm to the touch. Leave to cool in the tin for 5 minutes, then serve warm or transfer to a wire rack to cool completely. Spread a teaspoon of dulce de leche over the top of each muffin before serving.

185 Toasted almond & apricot muffins

100 g/3½ oz dried apricots, cut into
   small pieces
3 tbsp fresh orange juice
50 g/1¾ oz blanched almonds
280 g/10 oz plain flour
1 tbsp baking powder
pinch of salt
115 g/4 oz caster sugar

2 eggs
200 ml/7 fl oz buttermilk
6 tbsp sunflower oil or 85 g/3 oz butter,
   melted and cooled
¼ tsp almond essence
40 g/1½ oz flaked almonds

Place the apricots in a bowl, add the orange juice and leave to soak for 1 hour.

Preheat the oven to 200°C/400°F/Gas Mark 6. Line a 12-hole muffin tin with 12 paper cases. Preheat the grill and line a grill pan with foil. Spread out the almonds on the grill pan and toast until golden, turning frequently. Cool then chop coarsely.

Sift together the flour, baking powder and salt into a large bowl. Stir in the sugar and almonds.

Place the eggs in a large jug or bowl and beat lightly, then beat in the buttermilk, oil and almond essence. Make a well in the centre of the dry ingredients, pour in the beaten liquid ingredients and add the soaked apricots. Stir gently until just combined; do not overmix. Spoon the mixture into the paper cases. Scatter the flaked almonds on top of each muffin.

Bake in the preheated oven for 20 minutes, or until well risen, golden brown and firm to the touch. Leave to cool in the tin for 5 minutes, then serve warm or transfer to a wire rack to cool completely.

186 With apricot centres

Fill each paper muffin case halfway with mixture and spoon in a little apricot jam in the middle, then cover with the remaining mixture.

187 Tropical banana & passion fruit muffins

2 bananas
about 150 ml/5 fl oz milk
280 g/10 oz plain flour
1 tbsp baking powder
pinch of salt
115 g/4 oz soft light brown sugar
2 eggs

6 tbsp sunflower oil or 85 g/3 oz butter,
   melted and cooled
1 tsp vanilla extract
2 passion fruits
2 tbsp honey

Preheat the oven to 200°C/400°F/Gas Mark 6. Line a 12-hole muffin tin with 12 paper cases. Mash the bananas and put in a jug. Add enough milk to make the purée up to 250 ml/9 fl oz.

Sift together the flour, baking powder and salt into a large bowl. Stir in the sugar.

Place the eggs in a large jug or bowl and beat lightly, then beat in the banana and milk mixture, oil and vanilla extract. Make a well in the centre of the dry ingredients and pour in the beaten liquid ingredients. Stir gently until just combined; do not overmix. Spoon the mixture into the paper cases.

Bake in the preheated oven for 20 minutes, or until well risen, golden brown and firm to the touch. Leave to cool in the tin for 5 minutes, then transfer to a wire rack to cool completely.

Meanwhile, halve the passion fruits and spoon the pulp into a small saucepan. Add the honey and heat very gently until warmed through. Spoon on top of the muffins before serving.

Malted chocolate muffins

6 tbsp sunflower oil or 85 g/3 oz
butter, melted and cooled, plus
extra for greasing
150 g/5½ oz malted chocolate balls
225 g/8 oz plain flour
55 g/2 oz cocoa powder
1 tbsp baking powder
pinch of salt
115 g/4 oz soft light brown sugar
2 eggs
250 ml/9 fl oz buttermilk

ICING
55 g/2 oz plain chocolate, broken
into pieces
115 g/4 oz butter, softened
225 g/8 oz icing sugar

Preheat the oven to 200°C/400°F/Gas Mark 6. Grease a 12-hole muffin tin. Coarsely crush the chocolate balls, reserving 12 whole ones to decorate. Sift together the flour, cocoa, baking powder and salt into a large bowl. Stir in the brown sugar and the crushed chocolate balls.

Place the eggs in a large jug or bowl and beat lightly, then beat in the buttermilk and oil. Make a well in the centre of the dry ingredients and pour in the beaten liquid ingredients. Stir gently until just combined; do not overmix. Spoon the mixture into the muffin tin.

Bake in the preheated oven for 20 minutes, or until well risen and firm to the touch. Leave to cool in the tin for 5 minutes, then transfer to a wire rack to cool completely.

To make the icing, place the chocolate in a heatproof bowl, set the bowl over a saucepan of gently simmering water and heat until melted. Remove from the heat. Place the butter in a large bowl and beat until fluffy. Sift in the icing sugar and beat together until smooth and creamy. Add the melted chocolate and beat together. Spread the icing on top of the muffins and decorate each with one of the reserved chocolate balls.

Glazed honey muffins

6 tbsp sunflower oil, plus extra
for greasing
140 g/5 oz wholemeal flour
140 g/5 oz plain flour
1 tbsp baking powder
½ tsp bicarbonate of soda
½ tsp mixed spice
55 g/2 oz light brown sugar
100 g/3½ oz sultanas
2 eggs
200 ml/7 fl oz low-fat natural yogurt
8 tbsp clear honey

Place the eggs in a large jug or bowl and beat lightly, then beat in the yogurt, oil and 4 tablespoons of the honey. Make a well in the centre of the dry ingredients and pour in the beaten liquid ingredients. Stir until combined but do not overmix. Spoon the mixture into the muffin tin.

Bake in the preheated oven for 20 minutes, or until well risen, golden brown and firm to the touch. Leave to cool in the tin for 5 minutes, then drizzle 1 teaspoon of the remaining honey on top of each muffin. Serve warm or transfer to a wire rack to cool completely.

Preheat the oven to 200°C/400°F/ Gas Mark 6. Grease a 12-hole muffin tin. Sift together both flours, the baking powder, bicarbonate of soda and mixed spice into a large bowl, adding any bran left in the sieve. Stir in the sugar and sultanas.

190 Carrot cake muffins

6 tbsp sunflower oil, plus extra
for greasing
280 g/10 oz plain flour
1 tbsp baking powder
1 tsp mixed spice
pinch of salt
115 g/4 oz soft dark brown sugar
200 g/7 oz carrots, grated
50 g/1¾ oz walnuts or pecan nuts,
roughly chopped
50 g/1¾ oz sultanas
2 eggs
175 ml/6 fl oz milk
finely grated rind and juice
of 1 orange
strips of orange zest, to decorate

FROSTING
90 g/3¼ oz soft cream cheese
40 g/1½ oz butter
35 g/1¼ oz icing sugar

Preheat the oven to 200°C/400°F/ Gas Mark 6. Grease a 12-hole muffin tin. Sift together the flour, baking powder, mixed spice and salt into a large bowl. Stir in the brown sugar, carrot, walnuts and sultanas.

Place the eggs in a large jug or bowl and beat lightly, then beat in the milk, oil, orange rind and orange juice. Make a well in the centre of the dry ingredients and pour in the beaten liquid ingredients. Stir gently until just combined; do not overmix. Spoon the mixture into the muffin tin.

Bake in the preheated oven for 20 minutes, or until well risen, golden brown and firm to the touch. Leave to cool in the tin for 5 minutes, then transfer to a wire rack to cool completely.

To make the frosting, place the cream cheese and butter in a bowl and sift in the icing sugar. Beat together until light and fluffy. When the muffins are cold, spread the frosting on top of each, then decorate with strips of orange zest. Chill the muffins in the refrigerator until ready to serve.

191 With carrot decoration

Cut 6 ready-to-eat dried apricots in half and roll lengthways to form a carrot shape, place on each muffin and add green 'stalks' with pieces of angelica.

192 Gooey butterscotch cream muffins

150 g/5½ oz hard butterscotch sweets
280 g/10 oz plain flour
1 tbsp baking powder
pinch of salt
115 g/4 oz soft dark brown sugar

2 eggs
250 ml/9 fl oz double cream
6 tbsp sunflower oil or 85 g/3 oz butter,
melted and cooled

Preheat the oven to 200°C/400°F/Gas Mark 6. Line a 12-hole muffin tin with 12 paper cases. Place the butterscotch sweets in a strong polythene bag and hit with a meat mallet or the end of a wooden rolling pin until finely crushed.

Sift together the flour, baking powder and salt into a large bowl. Stir in the sugar and crushed sweets. Place the eggs in a large jug or bowl and beat lightly, then beat in the cream and oil. Make a well in the centre of the dry ingredients and pour in the beaten liquid ingredients. Stir gently until just combined; do not overmix. Spoon the mixture into the paper cases.

Bake in the preheated oven for 20 minutes, or until well risen, golden brown and firm to the touch. Leave to cool in the tin for 5 minutes, then serve warm or transfer to a wire rack to cool completely.

193 With butterscotch topping

Whip 175 ml/6 fl oz double cream with ½ teaspoon of vanilla extract, spread over the muffins, and scatter over 85 g/3 oz crushed butterscotch sweets.

2 tbsp instant coffee granules
2 tbsp boiling water
280 g/10 oz plain flour
1 tbsp baking powder
pinch of salt
115 g/4 oz soft light brown sugar
2 eggs

100 ml/3½ fl oz milk
6 tbsp sunflower oil or 85 g/3 oz butter,
    melted and cooled
6 tbsp coffee liqueur
50 g/1½ oz demerara sugar

Preheat the oven to 200°C/400°F/Gas Mark 6. Line a 12-hole muffin tin with 12 paper cases. Put the coffee granules and boiling water in a cup and stir until dissolved. Leave to cool.

Meanwhile, sift together the flour, baking powder and salt into a large bowl. Stir in the brown sugar. Place the eggs in a large jug or bowl and beat lightly, then beat in the milk, oil, dissolved coffee and liqueur. Make a well in the centre of the dry ingredients and pour in the beaten liquid ingredients. Stir gently until just combined; do not overmix. Spoon the mixture into the paper cases. Sprinkle the demerara sugar over the tops.

Bake in the preheated oven for 20 minutes, or until well risen, golden brown and firm to the touch. Leave to cool in the tin for 5 minutes, then serve warm or transfer to a wire rack to cool completely.

195 *With espresso icing*

Sift 115 g/4 oz icing sugar into a bowl, mix 1 teaspoon of espresso coffee powder with 1 tablespoon of boiling water, and add to the icing sugar, then mix until smooth and spoon over the muffins.

196 *Mocha muffins* MAKES 12

225 g/8 oz plain flour
1 tbsp baking powder
2 tbsp cocoa powder
pinch of salt
115 g/4 oz butter, melted
150 g/5½ oz demerara sugar
1 egg, lightly beaten
125 ml/4 fl oz milk
1 tsp almond essence
2 tbsp strong coffee

1 tbsp instant coffee powder
55 g/2 oz plain chocolate chips
25 g/1 oz raisins

COCOA TOPPING
3 tbsp demerara sugar
1 tbsp cocoa powder
1 tsp allspice

Preheat the oven to 190°C/375°F/ Gas Mark 5. Line a 12-hole muffin tin with 12 muffin paper cases. Sift the flour, baking powder, cocoa and salt into a large bowl.

Place the butter and demerara sugar in a separate bowl and beat together until light and fluffy, then stir in the beaten egg. Pour in the milk, almond essence and coffee, then add the coffee powder, chocolate chips and raisins and gently mix together.

Add the raisin mixture to the flour mixture and stir together until just combined. Do not overmix. Spoon the mixture into the paper cases.

To make the topping, place the demerara sugar in a bowl, add the cocoa and allspice and mix together well, then sprinkle the topping over the muffins.

Bake in the preheated oven for 20 minutes, or until well risen and golden brown. Leave to cool in the tin for 5 minutes, then serve warm or transfer to a wire rack to cool completely.

197 *With molten chocolate filling*

Omit the raisins from the mixture; you will need 100 g/3½ oz plain chocolate chips to make the centres. Spoon half the mixture into each paper muffin case and add a few chocolate chips to the middle, then top with the remaining mixture and bake as before.

100 g/3½ oz butter, softened
150 g/5½ oz caster sugar
115 g/4 oz soft light brown sugar
2 eggs
150 ml/5 fl oz soured cream
5 tbsp milk

250 g/9 oz plain flour
1 tsp bicarbonate of soda
2 tbsp cocoa powder
1 tsp allspice
200 g/7 oz plain chocolate chips

Preheat the oven to 190°C/375°F/Gas Mark 5. Line a 12-hole muffin tin with 12 paper cases. Place the butter, caster sugar and brown sugar in a large bowl and beat together, then beat in the eggs, soured cream and milk until thoroughly mixed.

Sift the flour, bicarbonate of soda, cocoa and allspice into a separate bowl and stir into the mixture. Add the chocolate chips and mix well. Spoon the mixture into the paper cases.

Bake in the preheated oven for 25–30 minutes. Leave to cool in the tin for 10 minutes, then transfer to a wire rack to cool completely.

250 g/9 oz rhubarb
125 g/4½ oz butter, melted and cooled
100 ml/3½ fl oz milk
2 eggs, lightly beaten
60 g/2¼ oz plain flour

2 tsp baking powder
125 g/4½ oz caster sugar
3 tbsp raisins
3 pieces stem ginger, chopped

Preheat the oven to 190°C/375°F/Gas Mark 5. Line a 12-hole muffin tin with 12 paper cases. Chop the rhubarb into lengths of about 1 cm/½ inch. Pour the melted butter and milk into a large bowl and beat in the eggs. Sift the flour and baking powder together and lightly fold into the wet mixture with the sugar. Gently stir in the rhubarb, raisins and stem ginger. Spoon the mixture into the paper cases.

Bake in the preheated oven for 15–20 minutes, or until the muffins are risen and golden and spring back when gently touched in the centre with the tip of an index finger. Leave to cool in the tin for 5 minutes, then serve warm.

200 *With yogurt icing*

Stir 1 tablespoon of ginger syrup into 150 ml/5 fl oz Greek yogurt and spread over the warm muffins.

Index